Inside Outer Space

INSIDE OUTER SPACE

SCIENCE FICTION PROFESSIONALS LOOK AT THEIR CRAFT

EDITED BY SHARON JARVIS

Frederick Ungar Publishing Co. New York

Copyright © 1985 by Frederick Ungar Publishing Co., Inc.

Inside outer space.

    Contents: There goes Deuteronomy / Parke Godwin ——
Goodbye Star Wars, hello Alley–oop / C.J. Cherryh ——
Historical hysteria or humour in science fiction /
Ron Goulart —— [etc.]
    1. Science fiction——History and criticism——Addresses,
essays, lectures. 2. Science fiction——Authorship——
Addresses, essays, lectures. I. Jarvis, Sharon.
PN3433.5.157   1985   809.3 876   84–28074
ISBN 0–8044–2411–X
ISBN 0–8044–6310–7 (pbk.)

CONTENTS

Introduction

Having been a book editor for years, I knew first-hand that it was no picnic. But being a book anthologist is infinitely worse. In trying to bring together a diverse assortment of contributors (myself included), one thing became evident: creative people do not operate on timetables.

But publishers do. That's a hard fact of life in this industry. (This axiom and others are explained elsewhere.) Fortunately, it all came together, and ten totally different people working in the science-fiction, fantasy, and horror genres have pooled their considerable talent and knowledge for this book. Although the contributors come from various areas of the genre, we are bound by a common love and dedication to a form of literature that actually makes us outcasts.

Much has been written and said, especially by Barry Malzberg and Harlan Ellison, about the "ghetto" of science fiction. The critics certainly don't pay us much attention, except when reviewing the latest *Star Wars* installment or making funny comments about Mr. Spock of *Star Trek*. They don't realize that the field of the fantastic does not necessarily include the Ewoks or the Enterprise. It does include Fredric Brown, Stanley G. Weinbaum, and H. P. Lovecraft—a long and rich history of fabulous literature being handed down through generations while other books—non-science fiction—flare in the limelight and then die.

There is also an incredible comradeship among people in this field that the average reader may not know about. This is the only genre where readers can actually meet and greet their favorite writers at one of the many local science-fiction conventions held each year throughout the United States. And most of the professionals in this field know each other by sight and by first name. Going to a convention can be like attending an annual class reunion or old home week, and the good fellowship evident at these gatherings permeates the pages of this collection. It is because of this comaraderie that I was able to put together this collection in the first place.

Each contributor was asked for an unusual approach to the genre, and the contributors were carefully chosen in order to cover a wide range of topics. The essays are not limited to writers and writing; other viewpoints and subjects are covered, forming an overall view of the field. Thus not only is the writer's viewpoint included but the publisher's and reader's as well.

Geo. Alec Effinger writes poignantly but humorously on the myriad problems a writer faces, from medical insurance to the IRS. Marion Zimmer Bradley delves into the pros and cons of fandom—those dedicated fans who feel a cultlike devotion to an author's works. And C. J. Cherryh punctures the *Star Wars* school of filmmaking by explaining scientifically how future wars will be fought, if at all.

The years Parke Godwin spent as an actor are put to good use now that he is a writer; Ron Goulart, known as the Mack Sennett of science fiction, graduated from writing cereal boxes; and Lloyd Biggle, Jr. and Marshall Tymn try to teach science fiction not only to their students but to other teachers.

I have also gone behind the scenes with my own essay, as does Stuart D. Schiff, as we reminisce about genre publishing both large and small. We've all tried to explore different aspects of the genre by discussing areas not covered before and by trying new approaches. It is our hope that these various essays will not only instruct and inform, but make you laugh, cry, and write outraged letters to your local congressperson.

The literature of the fantastic has produced classics and will continue to do so. Those of us associated with the field may have a love/hate relationship with it at times (witness Carter Scholz's searing essay on the science-fiction ghetto), but in the end, we acknowledge our debt to it.

My thanks and appreciation go to the many people who made this book possible out of a love for the field. It is a part of our lives, and we want to share that part with you.

—Sharon Jarvis

More often than not, Parke Godwin will explode into a room: his shock of white hair bobbing, his youthful face split by a grin. Most likely his shirt sleeves will be rolled up too. Parke has the kinetic energy of someone ready to fling himself enthusiastically into any project. As he usually does.

Back in the early 1950s, Parke was a fledgling writer with a number of published short stories to his credit. It wasn't until nearly twenty years later that he returned to the publishing scene with his first book, *Darker Places*, which was followed by a historical novel.

At this point, Parke had nary a thought for the science-fiction and fantasy fields until an old friend approached him with an idea. It was for a science-fiction novel set on a future Earth—a bizarre mix of religion, science, and witchcraft. Their collaboration resulted in his third book, the critically acclaimed *Masters of Solitude*, which is on its way to becoming a cult classic.

To date, Parke Godwin has a total of six books in print, two more to come, and a great many shorter pieces that have appeared in magazines such as *Fantasy & Science Fiction*, *Twilight Zone*, *Amazing*, and *Fantastic*. In 1982 he won the World Fantasy Award for Best Novella for "The Fire When It Comes," which has just been optioned for film. Currently he is involved with "dialog interviews" with people in the genre who usually don't get interviewed.

I first met Parke Godwin when I was an editor for Doubleday, acquiring science fiction and fantasy. He and his coauthor, Marvin Kaye, had submitted a proposal for a trilogy (which later became *Masters of Solitude*), along with part of the manuscript. I was greatly intrigued by the innovative setting and the lovely writing, but there were a number of problems to be ironed out. Both authors were invited to come to my office to discuss the situation.

It was a bit like inviting Laurel and Hardy to visit. Oh, I don't mean they destroyed the office with pratfalls and broken water mains, but they were a study in contrasts and both had an obvious theatrical flair. One was tall, one short. One was light, the other dark. Both were hams. Our conversations consisted of theatrical gentures accompanied by mellifluous voices (theirs). It turned out that their backgrounds were in theater and radio—which later came in handy when reading their new novel to convention-goers. In fact, watching them perform scenes from *Masters of Solitude* was sheer joy as their words came alive.

It was Parke's theater experience that gave me the idea for the following essay. I wondered if there were elements of acting and theater that could be applied to writing, and I posed the question to Parke. This delightful and informative essay is his answer.

1
THERE GOES DEUTERONOMY

PARKE GODWIN

I was eight years old when I thrust my first scribbled pages into my father's hand. He sighed and looked mournfully at my mother. "My God. Another writer."

It was the sound of compassion. Godwins have been writing, reporting, editing, or drawing for generations. One more grabbing a pencil was like one more Barrymore going on the stage: Jesus, can't he do *any*thing else?

My parents could and did. They were vaudevillians in the golden age of Schubert, Pantages, Keith-Orpheum, and Ziegfeld. The stamp never left them. I learned the taboos about whistling in dressing rooms and hats on the bed long before I knew the Ten Commandments—which to this day I can't run through without checking the script.

I grew up in a blizzard of pages, both my own and my father's, and went to sleep at night to the wheeze of his asthmatic old Oliver typewriter. Sitting across from me at the old-fashioned round dining table, he would edit a new radio script mumbling the lines and timing each page with a stopwatch. Comedy lines with the deft delivery of his years as straight man to a comic, fairy tales for children, blood and guts for *Gangbusters*, human interest for *Grand Central Station*, whose producer accepted one script with the delighted note: "This smells of greasepaint!"

So did my parents. Not surprisingly, so did I. When my fiction began to glimmer with more than boyish enthusiasm, Dad took me in hand and tried (oh, patiently!) to show me how to tighten, clarify, and cut. How to do the thing right. To be professional. To sell.

These sessions were liberal in their use of blue pencil, and only now do I realize what an act of love they were for my father. And how he must have felt when my first sale brought a check for several hundred dollars. My father rarely gushed. He didn't then.

"I'm proud that you've sold. Now, for God's sake, write *carefully*."

Prodigal I was, careful I was not. The pages flew, full of seething drama and what I thought was poetic truth or hard realism, but with no more shape than a circus fat lady. One agent responded to material I'd sent him with the advice, "You've got enough plot here for two novels. Pick some of it and find what it's about."

By then I'd tossed several sprawling Ur-novels into the trash and gone hooting off after the gypsy van of theater. Amateur and professional, in sickness and health, richer and lots poorer, I spent ten years as an actor. It was a love affair from the first. When the affair ended, the love remained. Still remains. And that's what this effusion is all about. There have been those writers who strongly influenced my work, but nothing has taught me so much about the art and business of writing as those ten years in theater. Nothing.

For openers, talent aside, consider something basic like survival. If you want to be an actor, you live in New York. Period. And in New York you can throw an agent out a window and hit thirty actors. In New York, any kind of artist learns survival first of all, or he quits. I registered with several office temporary bureaus and typed my way through most of the office buildings in Manhattan. Sometimes I lived on a loaf of bread and one or two cans of tuna fish for a week while making rounds and auditions. From direct experience, the rule is that one can keep going up to three full days without food before getting really weak. You don't get fat or feel very secure, but you can do it if you have to. You acquire the survival instincts of a rat. And gradually the jobs come.

Gradually I say, because along with survival, you add rejection to your daily diet like vitamins and learn to swallow it without a blink in order to get on to the next possibility. A professional actor at an audition wastes neither his time nor the director's. He does what's asked of him, leaves his photograph and resume, and heads off to the next stop in a busy day. He hopes he gets the job, assumes he won't, and doesn't worry one way or the other. The person interviewing him has seen hundreds that day. He may be encouraging or a snide little ass. The actor may have been shrugged off in a few seconds after waiting for more than an hour. If it gets to him, discourages him, blunts his attack on the next audition, he's dead. He learns to put a shell over his ego, when to assert it, and when to pack it away.

Project this to the writing business and think of the writers you've seen fulminating over one rejection of a manuscript. Think of the reams of paper that fanzines consume in intramural bitching, backbiting, and endless self-justification. If an actor wasted himself on that, he'd burn out in months.

Bad reviews are another side of the same bag. I've seen fine actors get the short end of a critic's praise and lesser performers praised to the skies. The worst review I ever got lauded the entire cast, singled me out as the lame exception, and then proceeded to eviscerate me. I read that review a half-hour before going out to try to make the audience laugh. Why not? That's what they paid for.

Reviews, good or bad, come with the territory. As soon as you stick your head up high enough to be noticed at all, someone's going to kiss you and someone else is going to throw a rock. The good reviews will help business, the bad one's won't hurt it that much, and both will balance each other out, so you won't sweat it. "When you start to believe your own reviews," my father said once, "you're through." You learn not to be impressed too much either way. You underline quotes that might look good on a marquee or a book jacket, and the hell with the rest. No one with half a mind will be impressed by them anyway.

One more fringe benefit, the most important: You learn to work, to pace yourself, to go the distance, to commit, to deliver. Two minutes late in an Equity rehearsal can dock your pay. The second infraction can get you replaced. Time is fleeting and actors legion. In a Shakespearean repertory company in 1969, our director opened rehearsals of *Macbeth* with the announcement, "Ladies and gentlemen, we have exactly forty rehearsal hours to mount this play." He read the cast list quickly and said then, "Okay, read through, please. Act one, scene one. Go."

We read through the play. Then the director flipped back to page one of his show book, handed it to the stage manager, and said, "We now have thirty-nine hours. Act one, scene one. Let's block."

Not unusual, in fact a mild example. In theater, as in publishing, panic and crisis are what you take with lunch. If you ever wondered *why* the show must go on, it's because everybody concerned—producer, director, actors, stage managers—is up to the neck in contracts. Money is involved, financial commitment. That's why they look for professionals, because pros don't fool around. They contract to do it, then figure out how, and then they damned well better deliver.

And all of this—to survive, to toughen, to live with rejection, to discipline and commit, to keep your body fit and your mind sharp—all of it is just openers to keep you in the game. But it's the hardest part. The buses are full of people, going back to Podunk, who didn't have that pair of Jacks to start. Because talent is not the trick. It's learning how to last, to go the distance in the loveliest art form, and the roughest business in the world.

The principle is transferable. There are hordes of people with something to say and the talent to say it. The buses are full of them, too. They couldn't go the distance, couldn't hack the rejection or the months and years of drudgery that writing a book requires.

Take a moment to listen to the cries at the Wailing Wall in publishing today. In our genre alone—fantasy and science fiction—any journal you pick up will tell you what's happening. The price of money is up, the fat times are over, editors are being axed right and left, advances are shriveling, the "mid-list" is a thing of the past, and everyone is playing it close to the chest just to hang onto their jobs.

It is to laugh, Charlie.

Just for the old sense of wonder, want to do some numbers the way theater does them? In 1957 William Gibson opened his *Two For The Seesaw* with Henry Fonda and Anne Bancroft for just over seventy-four thousand dollars. To mount the same show today, multiply that by ten, and that's a straight drama with a cast of two. For a musical, costs today will go over a million or even two million before the backers make a dime.

So what you open with has got to be the best, because "pretty good" closes on Saturday night. That was the rest of my education: what makes a good play.

A play is a delicate but smoothly functioning machine. Mistakes and indulgences tolerable in novels are instantly visible onstage. That's why all plays are essentially collaborations. The producer and director will want changes. If name actors are involved, *they'll* want changes. Because reputations and a great deal of money are on the line, they can't open with "pretty good." That's what you fiddle with out of town and during previews to make it work. The critics see the machinery at optimum. Or it folds with a net loss of hundreds of thousands.

So no one, least of all the playwright, can afford to kid himself about what he's got.

With every good play that I've seen or worked in, I asked myself: what made it go? And while there were different factors, one never changed. Economy—that cleared the debris from the script and left it free from distilled meaning and action. In a play as it happens before you, good and bad are kinetic. You can *feel* a scene or an act running ten or even five minutes too long. There's a palpable arc of involvement for the audience and it slumps very easily. You can *hear* a stretch of dialogue that doesn't go anywhere. The play has to be honed, tightened, or everyone concerned is unemployed again.

Tight became synonymous with good to me or at least a first step toward it. Next in line is *sound*. A play's characters tell the story in dialogue. That dialogue, plus the actors' insights, give you the underpinning of character. There must be recognizable human beings on the stage. Realistic or larger-than-life, they must proceed from a commonality of human experience. A great deal of an actor's basic training is in mining this common lode, bringing it out of himself, finding ways to articulate it in terms of the play and projecting it to a house full of people who have paid as much as fifty dollars for their seats. Would you spend that much on "pretty good" or go for the best?

The dialogue, the precise delineation of character and plot, all add to kinetic economy, the thing that keeps the audience watching and the reader turning pages. The problem, the conflict. As a young writer and student actor, this was very hard for me to learn. I grayed the temples of more than one director before I learned the simple rule of character I've followed ever since. In order to present (on page or stage) a character the audience and/or reader will believe in, you must give them someone they can identify with or at least recognize. To do this, you ask yourself (and then answer): *Who is he? Where is he going? What does he want?* You could write a lengthy monograph on those three questions in building a character, and Stanislavsky did, but they boil down to just that. And you have to know it.

This applies to scenes as well as the work as a whole. Whenever I'm stuck or up a wrong alley, I go back to the basics and find the *action* of the character. What's he doing in this scene? Is the scene itself necessary to development? Is there a better choice I haven't thought of? If the scene and the character's participation are necessary, I get even more basic, back to Acting 101. Where's he been just before this? Where's he going afterward? What time of day is it? How's he feeling? What's his relationship to the other characters in the scene?

There's no place where this is so needed as in delineation of conflict characters. If they don't work, the conflict and the story don't work. For a dreadful movie like *Conan*, they could (and did) get any muscular ham sandwich to play the hero. But James Earl Jones did the evil magician and Max Von Sydow did a cameo as an old king that blew the whole movie away.

If this is so on stage, why not on the page as well? Page-turning comes from involvement with the problem—which stems from its believability. While writing a major novel with Marvin Kaye, *The Masters of Solitude*, I had to introduce the lead "villain" Uriah into the story long after many strong characters had already been developed. Uriah couldn't be a pushover or a simplistic monochrome. The more depth and complexity Uriah had, the more convincing he'd be. So, in short, I created a character I'd love to play. First I found out who and what he was: Uriah was a man totally committed to the most rigid interpretation of Christian theology, diametrically opposed to the witchcraft religion of the hero, Arin, as an ultimate evil. He wanted the covens blotted out. Okay, think Cotton Mather and Torquemada.

Well, yeah . . . but isn't this simplistic? Just another witch-burner, another Jerry Falwell? Right, but what of the human being underneath these commitments? It would be easy to make Uriah a fire-eyed fundamentalist. The fire is there, to be sure, but controlled to laser intensity. I gave Uriah a keen intellect, a feeling for words (a relief after writing for the simple coven members) and a sense of irony. Although his beliefs and the needs of his people force him to a single course of action, his nature can't help seeing the gap between the ideal and the actual. And, forced to expedients as coldly practical as those of his opponent, Uriah continually falls back on the safety valve of irony.

And I discovered, rather than created in Uriah, a reluctant but instinctive liking for the hero Arin—so different yet so like himself in his aims.

"We have a great deal in common, Prince. For all your talk of warmth and love, and the sweaty self-delusion of your Circle, you have the makings of an exquisite bastard. You find coldness in me? I see it growing in you. It's not easy to carry a king's mission in this world or the next. And we both know that heroes have bad dreams that never find their way into songs."

Here Uriah is speaking for both of them and the lot given them by their world. He knows the natural result of vaulting intellect: vaulting ambition, stymied by his faith and commitments and suspected only by Arin.

"I envy you, Arin. You can go and become. I must stay and be . . . I want to be more."

The bond between them and the imbalance that leads to conflict make up the heart of drama. Uriah was a strong, intelligent man who did what he had to in order to achieve what he must. He is a villain only in relation to Arin's purposes. The CIA would recruit him in a minute.

Throughout my work there is the tendency, learned in theater, to play against the obvious colors of a scene. In *The Masters of Solitude*, there's a scene where what's happening is so gut-level horrifying that it was unbearable to write. To use Lovecraftian adjectives here would make it a page out of *Horror Tales* at its most fulsome. Without diluting the horror at all, I wrote the scene as black comedy à la Pinter in *The Birthday Party*. The horror is enhanced by underwriting or "playing against the scene."

Again, in my Arthurian novel *Firelord*, Trystan comes out of the hell of battle in adrenaline shock. He is laughing maniacally about being kicked by his horse in full view of his men and the enemy. He is *too* articulate, *too* glib, *too* lyrical for the circumstances, collapsing at Arthur's feet, helpless with laughter. Only in his last, tremulous line does the reader know what's under it all, the horror he must blot out with words and wit, any kind of sound. "Did you see the water in the shallows? It was pure red."

You don't have to play such obvious colors. You let them play themselves.

I've followed these basic principles of theater in everything I've written. I know a scene is basically sound if it types easily, that it's good when it gets up off the page and *plays*. I know the reader will care about a character when *I* know enough to care and put that caring on the page. One of the finest actors I've ever worked with was a tiny wisp of a man, a director's dream. Put him on a stage, tied to a chair in the middle of furious activity, Bill Preston would find something to make himself interesting. So I view characters carefully, even the walk-ons. Find something to give them, make them interesting, make them play. The reader occasionally welcomes a rest from the intensity of the main problem or the viewpoint character. In *Firelord*, the character Geraint is not central to the plot, entering only now and then. But he never just walks on, he *explodes* on with a torrent of energy, complacent faith and physical courage of a psychotic degree. He is an excellent foil for the most sensible Arthur. When told they are to be three men against eighty Saxons, Geraint only smiles blissfully.

"Do you not see the glorious mathematics of it? That's twenty-six apiece!"

As a main character, Geraint would wear you out and you'd have trouble believing in him. In support, he's volatile, hurtling, doomed—lovely.

Cutting is another inflexible rule of mine. I can't stand to see clear ideas and dialogue blurred with fat, so I try to cut every word that doesn't add to the effect, every dependent clause that holds up the forward thrust. The compulsion to cut and tighten may come from theater or it may be inherent. There's the ever-present memory of my father timing a radio script page by page with his stopwatch. A half hour show had exactly twenty-four minutes to tell its story. The other four belonged to the sponsor who got snippy if his time was curtailed, since he was paying for the whole half hour.

And there's the family legend of my grandfather, Harry Post Godwin, city editor of Washington's *Evening Star* around 1900. Apparently he had a church-and-obit writer who couldn't yell "fire!" in less than a thousand words. Harry rode the verbose chap mercilessly, slashed his copy in half, and rewrote the rest. One day the hapless C&O missed the large reference Bible from his desk and asked around the city room for it.

"Harry's got it," someone told him.

"Oh, God," the writer groaned. "There goes Deuteronomy."

One inviolate rule of vaudeville was: never tire your audience out. Always leave them wanting more.

Sadly, too many genre writers today have forgotten or never heard of the notion, which may show my advancing age. The hammered-in kinetic sense of pace and economy learned in theater was augmented by the writers I read and emulated myself in the early days. Most of them had theater or newspaper backgrounds. Ring Lardner, Dorothy Parker, and Robert Benchley cut their teeth on deadlines and the need to find the one right word to obviate three or four. Steinbeck could be effective with very few words. Sinclair Lewis, like Parker, could impale a whole character on the lance of a phrase. George Kaufman was a compulsive cutter, deleting every word that got in the way of his point or his laughs.

Unfortunately verbosity is fashionable now. Never write a paragraph if you can blow it up into a page. I'm at a loss to explain, much less to read, the spate of "over-writers" the last ten years have produced, particularly in science fiction and fantasy. Quite obviously, Tolkien is easier to read than to emulate—not for want of trying, God knows—and you can find imitation Dunsany on any book rack. Charmed by the deceptive simplicity of his prose, the young writer is lulled into believing that simplicity equals ease, the same delusion many tyros once had about the stream-of-consciousness novel. Not so—but they know by now, having tried, how tight those silken lines of Dunsany's are and how many wrong words were thrown out to make way for the right ones.

Part of the trend is a plain change of standard. I say change rather than degeneration to be fair, since different times have different frames of reference. I grew up in a time of faster-paced drama and prose. What I see now is not so much new as an attempted return to the indulgent rambling of the nineteenth century without the Victorian values or the subtle craft of, say, a James or Le Fanu. Evidently this new generation of readers will sit and digest 750 flabbily written pages without cavil. Certainly they'll sit through a space opera too long by forty-five minutes of visuals if there's big Dolby sound and a John Williams score soaring and sobbing from the speakers. Or a decayed corpse or two in close-up just to keep things *gemütlichkeit*. Subtlety is no longer the name of the game, but then these people were parked in front of a television set by their mothers and placidly watched Howdy Doody and Romper Room for so many years that they will now follow anything that moves and complacently do the same with a book.

Part of this trend is business. The packaging of books is still a gamble but with much less margin for error than in former years. As one editor told me, "A big book should look big. It should look important to get the attention it needs to justify its spot at the top of the list. If it's nine hundred pages, it looks and feels *important*." By this logic alone, the

Manhattan telephone directory could be a best seller. Not much plot, but look at the cast!

Such cases of literary elephantiasis, for sheer bulk, effort and price alone, will get critical attention. Sad to think what would happen today to a slim little masterpiece of forty thousand words called *Goodbye Mister Chips*. How would they package it?

And again my informative editor, never a woman to mince words: "Some writers become editorially untouchable." Meaning that good reviews, the adulation of fans, the heady lionizing at conventions, high royalties, etc. have made them stars. A suggestion to cut their pithy, iridescent prose is an insult to literature and good for at least a week's sulk and an astringent letter of comment by the wounded author in several fanzines.

An editor shouldn't have to demand cuts of a professional writer. The stuff should be cut and trimmed to clarity before the editor even sees it. That way the writer knows the choices are all his. It takes a little more discipline, a little more detachment, countless challenges to his own ego: Do I need this? Haven't I said it before? Is it that important? Is this dialogue as tight as it could be? But the pro knows exactly what that ego is worth on the market. Or should. If the material is an essential digression, the author, not the editor, should find a way to synthesize it with the main thrust of the work. Playwrights do. As seen above, they bloody well have to. Not to mention composers for whom synthesis is a basic tool. Why not a novelist? Well they did, forty or fifty years ago when writers took their work more seriously and themselves less. But they didn't go to science-fiction conventions whereas some of their successors seem to spend more time being literary personalities than writers.

Physician, heal thyself Department: honest friends have told me that *Solitude* suffered in part from just this bloat and I must shamefacedly admit it. The book took too long to get off the ground and fly. The same story today would take me much less time from start to heart. I've developed a better facility to ask: "Okay, what's this *about*?" While viewing with alarm, allow us to point with pride: once the plot mechanism was all set up, we used every means possible to montage and compact an enormous amount of material, cutting back and forth between the various plot currents flowing toward the climax. After the first third of the book, when we'd found our language and style and were no long groping our way, we had long Talmudic arguments on what *had* to go in. Everything else went in the trash.

In 1983 there was at least one very fine fantasy book on the *New New Times* best-seller list that would have been immensely improved by basic cutting. Not rewrite, not better choices; the author knows what she's doing. The book has magic and a music of its own, but the music is choked by a plethora of notes that blur and attentuate its true lines. Cutting in this case, as I wrote the author, would have entailed no loss of values, merely cleared away the repetitions, unnecessary clauses and verbal debris that bloated every page by about a third.

But . . . the publisher wanted a big book to fit a certain price slot, and for that you gotta give them lots of pages. So shut up, Godwin, what do *you* know about it?

I know what I see. I learned the uses of language in theater where it needs the sinew to work, not just lie there. I see prose getting flabbier and more self-indulgent. I see potentially good writing attenuated by bloat, lack of discipline, and an abysmal lack of *ear*. Maybe that's why I'd rather read a good short story in the genre than three of the most significant novels. And maybe this is why the market is dwindling. Perhaps others are beginning to yawn with me. When that happens in theater, you play your last act to an empty house. In publishing it takes much longer, but sooner or later the reader is going to know he got seven hundred pages of a three-hundred-page book and damned well resent it.

Perhaps when a tight new novel comes along with sufficient impact to be imitated, there'll be a lemming-rush toward concision again. I mean they can't just get fatter and fatter, can they?

Can they . . . ?

My first Shakespearan role as a student actor was Borachio in *Much Ado About Nothing*. It was a marvelous part with plenty of time onstage for invention and silken villainy. My enthusiasm ran riot. I invented so much in rehearsal that the director stopped me in protest.

"Look, what you've got is great, but there's too much of it. You got four different bits of *shtick* going in one scene. Pick one of them and get *on* with it."

That sat not well with me. I hated to kill my own children. "What's wrong with using all four?"

The director covered his eyes and slumped ever farther down in his seat. "Because the scene's not about that. And someone in the house may have to catch a train."

The *science* in science fiction has always been a bone of contention. For many years, it was argued that characterization and plot were sacrificed on the altar of technology. On the silver screen, science was ignored entirely. (Think of the totally impossible mating between humans and lizards in the television series *V*, for instance.)

And then there is *Star Wars*, which convinced generations that there was no greater excitement than Luke Skywalker gunning down evil ships of the Empire as the *Milennium Falcon* whizzes through space.

There is only one problem. According to Hugo-Award winning author C. J. Cherryh, it can't possibly happen.

In fact, most of those wonderfully thrilling battles in space, be it in books or movies, are scientifically inaccurate. And even more depressing, a real war in space demands more calculations than a Rubik's Cube and is about as exciting as watching your dog scratch fleas.

Make that a Neanderthal dog. . . .

2
GOODBYE STAR WARS, HELLO ALLEY-OOP
C. J. CHERRYH

Planets are a commodity of value at two stages of a humanoid species's existence: either as cradle or as retirement home. Otherwise taken, their value is negligible, and the preponderance of them—taken with moons, moonlets, asteroids, rings and such—might well be classified as navigational hazards rather than prizes of great value.

In any consideration of conflict, the first and most necessary question is easily: Why?

War is expensive. Contrary to all economic theories that equate war with boom periods and profit-making, technological war is a very expensive undertaking; and while an economic boom does often follow a war, it really issues from the research and development that produces new technology. A war generally produces economic disruption, particularly when the boom cools and the war debt comes due. A good research-and-development program is a much better substitute, even in purely practical terms. So if no technological power can contemplate war with another technological power without taking expense into account, what motives could override financial interest and drive a government to war?

Hope of even larger gain?

One of the most common scenarios for future war has been that of planetary conquest—outright aggression on the part of some technolog-ically superior civilization that finds it profitable to spend ships and lives taking someone else's world as base, mining station, or resort center. In my own estimation the resort center and new hotel complex is a more probable motive than the mining interest, for the reasons first stated: planets are not worth the effort except for a species in its infancy (at which stage it cannot travel in space to reach anyone else); or for some species not well suited to space (and why would they have gone to space in the first place?); or lastly for some incredibly rich, prolific, energy-wasteful spacefarers whose motives have become more hedonistic than practical.

The fact is that planets produce little that is unique, and certainly very little that would justify the expense of frequent dives into the planetary gravity well to bring the item out. Water, metals of all sorts, soil, light, power, agriculture—all these things are potentially more available in space than on a world, by the example of our own rather ordinary G class star. Artificial satellites can be built to contain farms that boast real dirt, with controlled growing seasons and regulated solar input from their star. Space stations can be aquatic or residential, can have interior land-scapes, or be whatever one desires. The detritus that likely orbits every star is full of source metals and minerals, as well as ice (hydrogen and oxygen), natural gas (methane), and so on, not mentioning, of course, the vast energy of the star itself to draw on. The only scenario in which planets could be universally valuable demands that our own solar system be quite unique, that the myriads of stars travel in total void unaccom-panied by useful debris and planets. However, considering the likely evolution of stars—condensation out of interstellar clouds—the reverse that all stars collect a great deal of junk about their waists, and travel with it, is more likely true. This junk consists of raw materials so abundant a thousand spacefaring species could plunder all they like and still not make a dent in the supply.

So why be interested in other worlds at all? Aesthetics, perhaps. The curiosity of them. But tourism is for the rich and idle, and pertains to older species.

That is why I say the motive for planetary conquest as resort develop-ment for hedonists is more likely than mining for a young and hungry civilization.

You will gather I do not particularly hold with conquer-the-planets tales. I just can't figure out why a species that has gotten out of its own native gravity well and gone interstellar in any big way will *ever* be motivated to use a planet other than as a source of exotica such as woods, perfumes, native crafts, artwork—in short, the things a planetary biology will produce. Or a planet can be used as a dumping ground, a prison, if you like, for individuals barred from the freedom of space. A planetary gravity well is not an easy thing to escape without truly advanced technology; access is easy to deny to a world, if you command the high ground—space itself. Ground-based insurrections can never reach a station without exterior help or a space program.

Earth, for instance, may discover that its real value in the universe consists of its unique arts, its thoughts, its coffees, teas, wines, and the patterns of its woods. Most of these items are fairly light and easy to get offworld, and might pay as trade goods.

But can woods from Earth outvalue those of Tau Ceti II? Perhaps. Perhaps not.

Can they be worth a war?

I doubt it.

So we return to the why of it. Why will people fight?

The possibility always exists, of course, of a cosmic misunderstanding, the encounter of two species with such widely divergent instincts that conflict occurs unwished by either side. But humankind, at least, has begun to discover, as a result of its advanced technology, that it is interdependent not only with its own kind, but also with semisapients and protozoa on its own planet. Humanity, in other words, has reached that level at which it can destroy life on its own planet, which is precisely the technological level at which it can escape the planet. As a natural concomitant to our own technological expansion, we are learning not only tolerance of other kinds, but their value. From being able to destroy the world, we must consciously and daily refrain. It seems reasonable that any species that hopes to get off its planet much reach such consciousness of power and responsibility . . . or kill itself off before it can get offplanet.

Random aggression is therefore a trait subject to severe culling *before* the starfaring stage, and must be somewhat rarer than some might suspect.

Purposeful aggression is subject to the same strictures.

It is possible, still, that there might be some aggressive species or totally xenophobic species which would seek war for its own sake.

And there may be other species, of course, who will have to study a long time to learn what the word war means at all, species whose patterns of aggression are very divergent from ours and so specific to particular situations that they are not species-threatening; or species whose responses are totally bizarre from our viewpoint.

With such beings, conflicts might take many shapes.

But with humanity?

A good many human motives for conflict may well disappear in a tomorrow of unlimited space and unlimited frontiers, where there is room for every opinion, no matter how divergent; and where resources are so unlimited that a ship in a single trip might fling about a power output equal to the total power output of a major nation of today, and count it as ordinary as we count our own airconditioned, heated homes—each one of which annually uses the total power expenditure of an ancient empire. In space, using such things as matter/antimatter conversion, we will not think high energy use that expensive; and even sublight voyages can be counted in less than decades.

Why would humans fight?

In self-defense, perhaps. For right-of-way to the stars, since specific narrow trade routes can conceivably be interdicted. For the right to get off a world. And sometimes, perhaps, though saddest, because two factions hold opposing ideas and refuse to separate from each other, despite enough room to do so.

The likeliest causes of future war are far more abstract things than worlds and resources, any of which can be picked up like pebbles on a free beach.

And the difficulties of fighting it at all—

Consider, for instance, a war in which not only the battle lines but the bases are constantly shifting. Even stars change positions relative to each other, and smaller bodies whirling at different rates about a single star do confound the planning.

Between stars, you really have to plan strategy in advance, launching your ships on runs that will take them an average five to ten years to complete. You will get information that is at least five years old. And ships at high velocities can come and go inside your "lines" completely undetected.

How do you retain control and command of your own forces when all a ship knows of its government or mission is what the captain says? After all, he or she is all the authority the crew sees for years.

How do you protect a solar system when a ship inbound at .9 cee travels so fast it can reach the sun from the Earth in about ten minutes and chase the wavefront of its own communications so close that it would arrive across ninety-three million miles only a minute behind its own message that it was inbound? Radar, of course, has to reach the object, bounce off, *and* return to the receiver before you can see it coming—so multiply that time by two before you know an attack is inbound. The ship gets there in half the time and strikes before your ships, moving relational to your station, have more than a minute's warning—less than time enough to get a defending ship under way.

And if your own ships are under way in another direction, they have to get rid of all their velocity before they can even begin to advance back toward the intruder.

So your planet/station/mining base was just struck—not with lasers: wasteful of energy. It's more efficient to boost up some cheap rock to .9 cee and let fly with it. Cannonballs. What doesn't burn up in atmospheric friction is going to hit with the kind of impact that formed the Arizona meteor crater and the one in Siberia. If you do that often enough near major cities, civilization is done.

One big rock and the climate may change—forever.

Of course you can leave a lot of debris flying through the system to take out station and ships as well. You can't see .9 cee missiles coming.

Not until they hit you.

So space war will be quite expensive if it is fought without rules, without conventions and limitations. Inhabited worlds cannot survive and ships-at-large cannot, on the average, be caught. Only the spacefarers might stand a chance. Sensible people may take to space and stay there, as remote from the area of conflict as possible, independent of all ties and, one would hope, learning something of wisdom about stones and glass houses.

Much more likely than all-out war is the local fracas, the diplomatic bluff, the showing of the gunboats.

Since this might probably cut off trade as nervous spacers run for far places, the war will soon develop boundaries and probably come to a negotiated settlement when the supply pinch makes itself felt. The only truly self-sufficient habitats—planets and large spacestations—will be the most nervous of all, and anxious to settle, since they can neither run nor fight with any hope of success.

Starships which can travel trans-cee will present different problems, opening up a great deal of territory in which ships can run and hide and render any far-flung government exceedingly unlikely if it does not rule with the consent of the governed. You simply can't control what you can't find, and if you're a stationary capital, it behooves you to remain on good terms with ships that can move and strike at will. Revolution might not even be necessary in a government too big to keep track of its pieces.

And ship-to-ship conflict?

First you have to find 'em . . . and that applies not alone to discovering which of fifteen hundred stars within forty light-years of earth was chosen by the ship you're hunting—or whether it's simply off in deep space, sitting and waiting. No, "finding 'em" can also apply to locating a ship in your own solar system.

If we were hunting an alien ship that arrived this instant within the perimeters of our own solar system, it might take over four hours for its deliberate signal to reach us. If it is traveling at .9 cee it can be well outside Pluto's orbit before we even knew it was there and gone. If it is trans-cee—no hope of finding it at all. And if we are two near-cee ships trying to fight each other in our solar system, a number of very strange things have to be taken into account.

Sublight, we all exist by Einstein's rules. Nothing in this space can travel faster than light. That's the law. If we stand imprudently EVA on the bow of a starship at .9999 cee and fire a pistol, we notice a disturbing phenomenon: the bullet will reach its relativistic limit instantly and hang there time-stopped just in front of us, infinitely massive because of its velocity (as are we) and traveling within our little packet of reality—because nothing in Einsteinian space can exceed cee. It and we go on together in the same moment. Explosive missiles or lasers fired just ahead of your bow reach your target less than .0001 split second before you do. You might as well ram the opposing ship as fire on their tail.

And if they're also going .9999 cee, you can't catch them in Einsteinian space.

If they're coming toward you, on the other hand, you'll never know it. Your radar can't pick them up in advance. Neither can anything else that depends on matter and particles. Take comfort. Odds do say in an area as big as a solar system you'll probably miss each other entirely.

If the enemy is behind you, you can fire missiles aft and let them fall back into their ship/time-packet/wave front. Things can drop *down* from cee.

Or if—an unpleasant scenario—you are equally matched in velocity and vector, i.e., running side by side, you can neither one turn nor escape the other, and you must simply hammer away at each other broadside like ancient frigates, since from each other's viewpoint, you're standing still.

Whatever you've fired off insystem, incidentally, does not "fall" or go away; it keeps traveling at the same speed. Forever. You might conceivably run into your own fire; and certainly you can run into friendly fire by accident, not to mention what the enemy lets off. Space battle will mean keeping track of every beam and projectile fired, no matter by whom or how long ago, because if you meet it at a great speed (yours or its)—just remember the way a .9 cee rock hits a planet. Big crater. No ship.

It is not a friendly act to dirty up someone's solar system with traveling projectiles and high-velocity rocks and go off and leave without telling the locals what the courses of these objects are. And it's expensive.

Considering that accelerating at 32 feet per second per second gives you the feeling of 1 gee, or Earth gravity, and that maintaining that thrust for 350 days gets you close to that .9 cee—at which point you would cross solar systems in hours, not the years needed by such craft as *Voyager*—you can see that velocity itself is both expensive and difficult to acquire. Without exotic technologies it takes time for a ship to get up to speed; and it takes an equal time at the same rate of deceleration to get rid of that speed when you arrive. So defending pilots can hardly scramble to meet attack. Nor can they orbit the system at high speeds while just waiting: such velocities do not lend themselves to circular maneuvers. Even if they might do it, Murphy's Law puts them clear across the system when an attack comes.

No defense possible, unless one can contrive to place obstacles large enough to deter an incoming ship from reckless speed.

An already "dirty" system, full of rocks and obstacles, might be the best protected against such intruders, but this might also discourage incoming traders, with some disadvantage to the system, one supposes. Expensive again—for any species.

Wars *on* planets, now. . . .

Environmentally expensive, to be sure.

An interstellar government might be disposed to cut off the offending planet from contact with the outside and let the locals settle it, dealing only with the winner. But on past human record, since one's internal enemies often seem to exploit a civil war, the government might instead decide to stop it in a hurry, which might in turn require ground forces in a very old-fashioned, nasty sort of conflict—in which indubitably the locals would have the advantage of terrain, and in which outsiders taking one side over the other might discover certain political consequences, and debts, and future problems.

So planetary civilizations might be liabilities to an interstellar civilization in many regards, considering, in prime, their diversity of terrain and their capacity for generating disputes over limited resources and for putting dissident groups territorially adjacent to each other. On such rocks might whole stellar civilizations founder, bogged down in endless petty wranglings by populations whose concept of horizons is limited by their seasons and their sky.

Cutting off warring planets entirely is probably the more prudent course, until they go to space on their own and have to be dealt with face to face, angry because you failed to help.

In the same way, contacting planet-bound aliens might well be a counterproductive act, embroiling the spacefarer in local situations and local factions, particularly when the species is physiologically capable of space flight and has not yet achieved it: this would indicate a primitive or, alternatively, mentally different culture, either one of which holds hazards.

Contacting a spacefaring culture might most likely be done initially through communications monitoring, simply listening for who else might be Out There, as they might be listening for us. And the knowledge that such a contact was made sight unseen and was now traveling toward human space might well test the qualities of human tolerance and xenophilia.

There remains, for cause of war, always the act of a lunatic, a pirate, a dissenter, or an entity with motives arising from nonhuman biology and culture. And that might entail one of the most difficult of decisions—to determine whether the isolated ship attack that took out New Chicago was the act of a lunatic, a prankster, a criminal, or the calculated policy of a nonhuman government which might differ in biology, mentality, and motive from anything ever encountered.

Military strategy depends on certain assumptions, one of the most basic of which is that we are fighting others who respond to the same stimuli and react predictably. Consider all these possibilities:

A feint might bring all-out attack.

Not to make a feint might cause the potential enemy to consider us an easy mark and might bring all-out attack.

To accept the damage might put us at moral advantage with the alien authorities.

To fail to avenge the attack might be dangerous.

The attack must be returned in exact measure as given to induce respect.

The attack must be returned a hundredfold because we will not get another chance.

The enemy has no allies and does not understand negotiation at all.

The enemy is a primitive member of a vast alliance embracing fifteen hundred star systems and employing technology far in advance of ours.

The aliens are retaliating in a measured way for damage accidentally inflicted by the contact team. They do not treat individual death as important, basing their own selfhood on the social unit, and they do not comprehend the extent to which humanity resents the loss of New Chicago.

The aliens have no social unit. Reproducing by fission, they are absolutely solitary and were brought into space by imprudent traders. Now they commit totally random actions, each according to its peculiar mindset. Only that very distant trader-species can deal with them.

Consider, too, that such divergent possibilities extend down to the tactical level, and that the type of ship and the capacity of their crews and equipment to stand certain stresses might be vastly different from human limits.

Interspecies war might be the most expensive of all, and very possibly without sensible or understandable issues. In such a war, humankind might never know why it had been fought, or even, at the conclusion, which side had won.

Or they might just go away.

In such considerations, do we sent out our probe ships armed or unarmed? In what posture do we meet the universe at large?

Voyager and *Pioneer* are our answers—encouraging answers, giving cause for optimism. Our experiences have made us wary but not utterly distrustful.

Trade is really humanity's favorite occupation, offering as it does the freedom to come and go in interesting places and deal with new things— and still come back to some kind of stranger-free home base, be it ship, station and world, or just a thoroughly familiar region of space that humanity calls its own.

We like to go *outside* our homes to meet strangers; those we invite inside are fewer. One wonders how we, ourselves, will react if others want to travel inside that space we define as ours—be it world or territory—to come and go at will.

Then we may find out what we really are.

Why doesn't anyone take humorous science fiction seriously?

No, this is not a trick question. It's actually an accurate reflection of the marketplace of the last decade or so. If you had to name some humorous science-fiction writers, you'd be hard pressed to come up with a list larger than the fingers of one hand, and you might not even think of that many.

I thought first of Ron Goulart, known as the Mack Sennett of science fiction, primarily for his consistency and longevity. There's also Isidore Haiblum, who has a fondness for Yiddish aliens, Robert Vardeman, who prefers lecherous genies and bumpkin heroes, and John Morressy, who writes short stories about an inept wizard married to a frog. There's also Joan Winston, the Erma Bombeck of *Star Trek*, but to die-hard science fiction fans, *Star Trek* doesn't count.

I also thought of Fredric Brown, but he's dead.

In fact, most of the humorous writers whom Ron Goulart mentions in his very personal essay have faded away, gone out of print, or died. The state of health of funny science fiction could be considered terminal . . . if it wasn't so funny. Fortunately, thanks to the roller coaster American economy, the situation may be changing, as depressed readers clamor for more entertainment. Ron may actually find his sales figures rising after all these years.

There's one interesting—and humorous—coincidence to all this. When Ace Books reprinted Ron Goulart's first funny science fiction novel, I was not only his copyeditor, but I wrote the blurb too. You may not have realized that, Ron ol' buddy, but it's too late to do anything about that now. . . .

3

HISTORICAL HYSTERIA OR HUMOR IN SCIENCE FICTION

RON GOULART

It occurs to me, after having typed the above title, that it might make a nifty one for a blank book. I also find myself, in undertaking to tackle this particular topic, feeling like the spokesperson from some obscure minority group (one that nobody's even bothered to make up slurs about) or some nearly lost cause. But since it's alleged that I write funny science fiction, I suppose it's my duty to speak up. I'm going to approach the subject more as a practitioner than a historian. So, while I'll drop names, there won't be a checklist of watershed works from Frank R. Stockton to Robert Sheckley and Kurt Vonnegut.

I first encountered humorous science fiction, during my long-ago youth, in a format that provided lots of colored pictures along with it: it was in the comic books of the late 1930s and early 1940s. People like Jack Cole, Basil Wolverton, Siegel and Shuster, C. C. Beck and Otto Binder and Alfred Bester were drawing and/or writing works of fantasy and science fiction that mixed action, violence, slapstick, burlesque and maybe even a little satire. Cole wrote and drew Plastic Man, one of my favorite superheroes of the period. Wolverton, both in his allegedly straight features like Spacehawk and wacky ones like Powerhouse Pepper, was always far from serious. Although Siegel and Shuster's Superman wasn't usually a laugh riot, they and their staff did get in some funny stuff now and then—particularly when dealing with a whimsical villain known as the Prankster. I still fondly recall the episode in which the Prankster managed to copyright the alphabet and then charged all book, magazine, and newspaper publishers outrageous fees for its use. When one smug publisher announced that he'd outwit the scheme by publishing a magazine that was all pictures, the Prankster merely smirked and inquired, "What'll you call it?" Beck and Binder, most of the time, turned out the adventures of the original Captain Marvel (the red-suited fellow who was Billy Batson in everyday life) and explored time travel, space travel, teleportation, the fourth dimension and just about every other basic pulp science fiction convention known to man, and never in a serious vein. Bester, in the days before *The Demolished Man*, wrote about a costumed little guy named Genius Jones. Possessed of no powers, Genius lived by his wits and an encyclopedic memory.

The drugstore I haunted in my youth and young manhood was catholic when it came to the variety of cheap thrills available on its stands. In addition to comics there were pulps, digests, paperbacks, and sundry other forms of paper ephemera. Therefore I was eventually able to widen my reading to stuff like *Thrilling Wonder, Startling Stories, Planet Stories*, the *Avon Fantasy Reader* and, eventually, *Fantasy & Science Fiction* and *Galaxy* without going further than three blocks from home. Donald A. Wollheim was an early contributor to my deliquency by introducing me to the works of Stanley Weinbaum in my youth, by way of *The Pocket Book of Science Fiction* and the *Fantasy Reader*. It was therein that I first discovered stories like *A Martian Odyssey*. I suppose it's only fitting that Wollheim's been stuck with the task of issuing more of my science fiction novels than any other publisher.

From Weinbaum I learned that you could do a funny story that wasn't a parody, one where the humor came out of the situation and the characters' reactions. I think, without bothering to dig out my Weinbaum collection, that he was the source of the "reluctant agent" gimmick that I've used frequently. That's where the focal character is sent to some wretched planet to fulfill a mission he's convinced will be painful if not out-and-out fatal. Of course, Bob Hope (in 1940s movie comedies like *My Favorite Blonde* and *Ghost Breakers*) was also an exponent of the reluctant hero approach.

In the pages of the pulps and digests I encountered Henry Kuttner (under most of his names), Fredric Brown, Anthony Boucher, C. M. Kornbluth, Damon Knight, L. Sprague de Camp and, eventually, Robert Sheckley. And in *Fantasy & Science Fiction* such lesser known but equally gifted writers as Will Stanton and Alan Nelson (his story *Narapoia*, about the man who believes people are plotting behind his back to do him good, was one of my favorites). I also discovered Ray Bradbury in my teens and was sidetracked into trying to write soulful, sensitive, poetic self-pitying science fiction yarns. Or at least fragments thereof. This impulse to create beautiful and serious science fiction, like acne, eventually passed.

By the time I went through the Bradbury phase, I'd already been writing for several years. And quite early on, while reciting one of my efforts to a grade-school class audience, I came to realize how gratifying laughter could be. In fact, most of the years I was striving to become a writer of short stories I was also showing up at various school affairs to do a stand-up comedy act. That meant I had to juggle my time so I could do my homework and still fit in time for drawing the cartoons I was certain would soon win me fame and fortune.

During my final year in high school I became aware that Anthony Boucher, who also resided in my native Berkeley, was going to be teaching a writing course in his home one evening a week. He and J. Francis McComas had only recently begun editing *The Magazine of Fantasy & Science Fiction* and I figured that all I had to do was show up at a class with a couple of my yarns and I'd come away with a contract and a check. It didn't work out quite like that, although I did sell my first story to Boucher a couple of years later. Had I grown to manhood in what we California outlanders referred to as Back East, the idea of a magazine editor's actually living in the same town probably wouldn't have seemed an unusual and exciting as it did to me. I'm surprised, after looking up Boucher's dates, to realize he must've been only in his late thirties when I first met him. At the time he seemed very old and wise to me, as well as comfortably avuncular. Boucher, unlike a few editors later encountered, never suggested I sober up and give more serious science fiction a try. He was more interested, as a teacher and an editor, in getting me to do what I wanted to do as effectively as possible.

By the time I entered college, despite dreams of glory in which I successfully pursued a career as an artistic triple threat—cartoonist, actor, writer—I decided to play it safe and go after a teaching credential. Fortunately I was wooed away into the advertising game before I got around to doing the necessary graduation work. One of the things I got out of majoring in English was a fascination with the picaresque novel as practiced by such British funny fellows as Fielding, Smollett, and Dickens. By utilizing the university's vast and impressive library, and by haunting the many second-hand book stores that flourished in the Bay Area at the time, I became familiar with such humorous writers as Nathanael West, P. G. Wodehouse, Robert Benchley, F. Anstey and E. Nesbit. These last two were special favorites of Boucher, who touted them to me.

Anstey is remembered today, if at all, for *Vice Versa*, a fantasy novel in which a father and his schoolboy son exchange bodies. I found his short stories particularly interesting. One such, *The Gull*, deals with a chap who becomes convinced his lady love, supposedly lost at sea, has come back as a seagull. Those of you who've read a story of mine called *Groucho* are aware of how I approach a similar notion.

I suppose this is as good a place as any to confess I also dipped into Thorne Smith's comedy-fantasy novels during my formative years. I didn't read such works as *Topper* and *Turnabout* (Smith's version of *Vice Versa*) from cover to cover, though, being interested then only in what the cover copy alluded to as the ribald passages. If memory serves, Smith wasn't that amusing. My only real regret when I recall his works is that I never did learn quite how to pronounce ribald.

I began selling in the science-fiction field when I was nineteen. For years I turned out only short stories and parodies. The parodies, by the way, were most often of writers I'd taken seriously only a few years earlier—Edgar Rice Burroughs, Lovecraft, Sax Rohmer. I was wary of tackling a novel, especially a funny one. Doing 180 or so pages of humorous science fiction struck me as about as hard as standing up and doing an eight-hour comedy monologue. It wasn't until I was in my early thirties, and safely married, that I made any sustained effort to do novels. A couple of earlier attempts, for which I'd whipped up sample chapters and an outline, hadn't fared well. The agent I had at the time wouldn't even offer one of them, fearful it might damage his reputation. The other did finally see print, thanks to my chum, William F. Nolan, as a novella. Under the title *Nesbit* it ran in the short-lived magazine *Gamma* and as *The Whole Round World* in an anthology of Nolan's. I was struck, when I came to revise the thing for the second go-round, at how much better I'd become since doing the first version. The plot has to do with a gorilla who has a human brain. . .

The Sword Swallower, which takes place in my Barnum System of planets and stars Ben Jolson of the Chameleon Corps, was my first published novel. But before Doubleday brought it forth in 1968, it had appeared in novelet form in *Fantasy & Science Fiction*. I did the ten thousand word version first to see if I could sustain a longer story. The format I used was the one I'd become fond of back in college, that of the picaresque. That seemed to work for me and I had wandering heroes in my next novels, *Gadget Man, After Things Fell Apart*, etc.

The danger in finding a workable format, especially if you've been hunting for one for years, is in sticking with it from then on. The films of the Three Stooges, to give but one example, illustrate some of the terrible side effects of this dogged approach. My own rule is never to write the same novel more then ten times, which explains why in recent years I've been attempting something beside planet picaresques and after-the-collapse future earth quests. Novels like *Cowboy Heaven*, wherein an android actor is brought in to substitute for an ailing John Wayne-type superstar, *Skyrocket Steele*, dealing with the making of a science fiction serial in Hollywood in 1941, and *The Prisoner of Blackwood Castle*, which is the sort of thing Anthony Hope might've done had he been moved to write in 1890s private detective horror/fantasy, have all been attempts to avoid the expected.

And, of course, I also work in other areas, turning out funny mysteries (*Ghosting, A Graveyard Of My Own*), funny Westerns and, twice, funny Regency romances. Lately, in such publications as *Twilight Zone* magazine, I've been doing funny nonfiction, mostly of a nostalgic turn. Like any self-respecting comedian, I want to believe I can work anywhere.

I remember reading someplace that Robert Benchley was moderately embarrassed by the fact that when he went to the movies and saw himself on the screen, he laughed louder and more appreciatively than just about anyone else in the audience. That gave me strength, or at least a foundation upon which to build a rationalization. Because I, too, am my own greatest fan. By the time a short story, article or novel has made it into print, and that may be as long as a year of more after the writing, it's almost always fresh and new to me. When I sit down to read one of my own works, I can be heard chuckling, giggling and, occasionally, slapping my knee. I'm certain that if I weren't me, I'd be a fan of me.

Neither idolaters nor denigrators of my work have ever been much flimflammed by what I concoct and pass off as science fiction. Here, for example, is a quote from the introduction to a story of mine in Jack Dann and Gardner Dozois's *Magicats!* "Ron Goulart has long been one of the funniest writers in science fiction, with an unerring instinct for all that is bizarre, zany, cockeyed, gonzo, and just plain *weird* in contemporary society." They know the short stories and novels are extrapolations not from the latest scientific breakthrough but from this morning's political and show business follies. The truth is that although I actually have been inspired by articles in *Scientific American*, much better sources are *The New York Times* and the *National Enquirer*.

I might also mention, with a sigh of fond regret, what a splendid source of inspiration Richard M. Nixon was to me. Having been born and raised in California, I'd had the extra advantage of being able to savor him several years before the nation as a whole. But it was the Nixon of the years just prior to and including Watergate who proved to me the most useful. I got at least one planetary novel, *A Whiff of Madness*, and one future Earth opus, *The Panchronicon Plot*, out of him.

I have no secrets to impart to would-be producers of zany science fiction. It's been my experience that being funny is either easy or impossible. If you have a knack for humor, and that may be caused by a genetic defect or some as yet phantom virus that strikes in childhood, all you can be taught is how to package your stuff more effectively. Even then, the most useful lessons are usually self-taught. You try out different techniques and approaches until you find what works best for you. Although audience response, in such forms as an editor's acceptance letter, a check, or a perfumed letter from a young lady fan who thinks you're awfully droll, helps, you are really the only true judge of what succeeds. You know when the story feels right.

And on that pontifical note, I'll shuffle off the stage to make way for the next act.

The acclaimed magazine *Whispers* first made its appearance over a decade ago in 1973. It continues to be published at the irregular rate of one and a half issues a year—depending on its editor/publisher Stuart David Schiff, who prefers the term irregular rather than erratic—and it continues to garner World Fantasy Awards in the process.

In 1977, Stu began Whispers Press, which has published about half a dozen books, including *Rime Isle* by Fritz Leiber, and the only hardcover edition of Robert Block's *Psycho II*. He also edits the *Whispers* anthology series for Doubleday, every one of which has been nominated for a World Fantasy Award.

As you can tell, *Whispers* and Whispers Press is primarily dedicated to horror and dark fantasy. And it must have been at a World Fantasy convention that I first met Stu Schiff; I can't remember exactly, because Stu is one of those people you think you've known all your life. On the other hand, how many people do you know who keep an eyeball in a jar? "Here's looking at you," Stu jokes. He got the eyeball in dental school where he was supposed to dissect it, but he found a better use for it. . . .

Although he gained hands-on experience as a small press publisher by actually publishing *Whispers*, Stu's historical knowledge of the field is extensive, as he demonstrates here. As a dedicated collector—books, artwork, magazines, manuscripts, letters, etc.—he cites names and dates, fact and figures, attesting not only to the glory years of small presses, but leading to some cautious conclusions about the future of this vanishing field.

4

THE GLORIOUS PAST, ERRATIC PRESENT, AND QUESTIONABLE FUTURE OF THE SPECIALTY PRESSES

STUART DAVID SCHIFF

Specialty-press publishing in the fantasy and science-fiction field may be defined as a person or small group of persons banding together in order to see fantasy or science-fiction books through from their manuscript stage to the published product. While this is certainly not unique to the fantasy and science-fiction field, I believe that the quality of authors and work our noncommercial presses produced was unique for a long period. It does not take much research to find that Robert Heinlein, Isaac Asimov, Ray Bradbury, Robert Bloch, Howard Phillips Lovecraft, Robert E. Howard, Fritz Leiber, Clifford Simak, Ted Sturgeon, and other very important fantasy and science-fiction writers, had their first or major works appear from the specialty presses. Why, though, did specialty presses originate?

The beginning point for the fantasy and science-fiction field's speciality publishers can be pinpointed to the depression years; therefore, it is conjectured that the depression helped create the speciality presses. I tend to agree with this. With the poor economic conditions, printers had the time, indeed, the need, to take on lesser-paying jobs in order to pay the bills, and some of the first specialty-press publishers used this route. Still, I feel the major reason for the presses' emergence was a *need* for the books rather than an opportunity to utilize silent presses. The need was there and commercial publishers were either unwilling to take the risks of the venture or unaware of the need. When did the forces necessary to create the fantasy and science-fiction presses come together to generate this phenomenon?

Although there is no complete agreement among the "experts," my feelings as to the field's first speciality press "book" is Allen Glasser's *The Cave Men of Venus*. This seventeen-page, soft-cover pamphlet was printed in 1932 by Conrad H. Rupert for Solar Publications of Jamaica, New York. Solar Publications, as well as the later and better known ARRA Printers, were the book-publishing arms of *Science Fiction Digest* (later *Fantasy Magazine*). This early science-fiction fan magazine (today termed "fanzine") was the result of several people to include Rupert, Glasser, Julius Schwartz, and Mortimer Weisinger (yes, this is the same Mort Weisinger of Superman fame). Some of these men had also had a hand in the two earliest fanzines, 1930's *Comet* (later *Cosmology*) and 1932's *The Time Traveller*. All of these magazines are worthwhile and interesting collectibles as are the Solar and ARRA booklets. Beside the Glasser item, other books produced by these people included Weisinger's *The Price of Peace* (1933), Abraham (A. A.) Merritt's *Thru the Dragon Glass* (1933), and Dr. David H. Keller's *Wolf Hollow Bubbles* (1934).

Some of the purists out there may be saying that soft-cover pamphlets are not "books." I strongly disagree but offer to you the first hardcover book in the fantasy and science fiction specialty-press field as being Eugene George Key's *Mars Mountain* (1935). This monumental (and unreadable) volume was published by Fantasy Pubs (Fantasy Publications), one William L. Crawford of Everett, Pennsylvania. Crawford had previous "book" credits with 1934's sort-of-untitled (the cover merely listed the two stories) softcover "anthology," "The White Sybil" (*sic*) by Clark Ashton Smith with "Men of Avalon" by David H. Keller. He had also previously published the now-rare magazines, *Unusual Stories* and *Marvel Tales*. Beside the infamous *Mars Mountain*, Crawford's claim to fame are as publisher of Howard Phillips Lovecraft's first truly-published book, *The Shadow over Innsmouth* (Visionary Publishing Company, 1936) and as 1947's founder of Fantasy Publishing Company, Incorporated (F.P.C.I.).

With the specialty presses' earliest benchmarks behind us, let me take a little time to talk about the collecting of specialty press books in the fantasy and science-fiction field. It has been shown by some investment experts that collecting first edition books and similar literary entities is one of the best ways to invest your money. An important first edition tends to appreciate in value ahead of inflation and most other investments. While a fine copy of *The Shadow over Innsmouth* in dust jacket may not bring the same auction prices as prime copies of Joyce's *Ulysses*, I have seen that particular book sell for over two thousand dollars. And recent sales of science fiction books at prices from five hundred to five thousand dollars have occurred in both auctions and book catalogs. In other words, collecting specialty-press books in this field can be done for both fun and profit. I do not intend to turn this essay into a price guide or claim it is anything close to a complete listing of all the collectible specialty-press books, but I will try to mention as many important books as I can while fulfilling this essay's aim to display and explain this interesting publishing phenomenon.

With that in mind, I would like to note three other major items published by the fantasy and science-fiction specialty presses during the years 1933–36. The first was Clark Ashton Smith's initial short story collection, *The Double Shadow and Other Fantasies* (1933). This may not fit some people's definition for a specialty press as it is believed that the publisher was Smith himself (no credits are given). Still, it was a masterful collection by a major fantasist. The second item on my list is Stanley Weinbaum's *Dawn of Flame and Other Stories* (The Milwaukee Fictioneers, 1936). This 250-copy edition was a memorial tribute to Weinbaum. Rupert was again the printer and the Milwaukee Fictioneers and the Milwaukee Chapter American Fiction Guild were fans and professionals who put the volume together. The third important book produced during this period was not a book at all, but rather seventeen unbound signatures issued as supplements to the *Science Fiction Digest* (later *Fantasy Magazine*). Titled *Cosmos*, this round-robin novel featured contributions by John W. Campbell, Jr., Abraham Merritt, Edmond Hamilton, E. E. Smith, and others. A rare cover (by the later-famous artist, Hans Bok) and table of contents pages were issued later to make this an unbound book.

In the years 1936–39, several important fanzines (such as *Imagination* and *The Science Fiction Critic*) were published, but no specialty press turned out a major title until 1939 when August Derleth and Donald

Wandrei's newly founded Arkham House published Howard Phillips Lovecraft's *The Outsider and Others*. Despite initial poor sales, this volume turned out to be one of the specialty presses' pivotal, if not *the* pivotal, books. It was important in two ways. Firstly, it was Arkham House's first book, and, in my opinion, Arkham House is *the* field's specialty press. Secondly, it is the book that initially gave Howard Phillips Lovecraft his reputation outside of the small coterie of *Weird Tales* fans. And it was Lovecraft's fame and collectibility that has rubbed off on the rest of the field's authors and presses.

Speaking of other specialty presses helped by the Lovecraft phenomenon, this book's editor followed the well-known axiom that "it takes one to know one" when she asked me to expostulate on the specialty presses of fantasy and science fiction. For those of you who do not know me, I am the publisher-editor of *Whispers* magazine and the Whispers Press. While I cannot lay claim to having been around when it all began or having typeset, printed, folded, and bound my publications by hand, I have done more than my share of hard (and hand) work with my hobby and experienced at-least-my-share of the problems that befall those unwary enough to attempt the "rewarding" life of the specialty-press publisher. My press's first planned book, *A Winter Wish* (1977), was authored by Lovecraft.

Getting back to Arkham House, August Derleth (who later became the firm's sole owner) often mentioned that it did not make a profit for many years. In fact, he many times mentioned that he had had to put thousands of his own dollars into Arkham House before it turned a profit in the 1950s. Although not a financial success for over a decade, it was still a huge literary success through its publishing of a remarkable number of first (and major) books to include volumes by Ray Bradbury (*Dark Carnival*, 1947), Robert Bloch (*The Opener of the Way*, 1945), Fritz Leiber (*Night's Black Agents*, 1947), Henry S. Whitehead (*Jumbee and Other Uncanny Tales*, 1944), and A. E. van Vogt (*Slan*, 1946). Other classics they published during those formative years included works by Clark Ashton Smith (*Out of Space and Time*, 1942; *Lost Worlds*, 1944), Frank Belknap Long (*The Hounds of Tindalos*, 1946) William Hope Hodgson (*The House on the Borderland and `Other Novels*, 1946) Robert E. Howard (*Skull-Face and Others*, 1946), Donald Wandrei (*The Eye and the Finger*, 1944), and Lord Dunsany (*The Fourth Book of Jorkens*, 1949). It is difficult to believe that these prestigious books did not earn Arkham House immediate financial success, but that was what occurred.

As the years went by, *The Outsider*'s fame grew. While Arkham House continued to publish books by Lovecraft, Derleth, Smith, and others, they also produced early books by Carl Jacboi, Vincent Starrett, Joseph Payne Brennan, Manly Wade Wellman, Ramsey Campbell, and the like. Indeed, Arkham House put the field's specialty presses on the track and kept them there.

If I may intrude upon my own essay, let me note that I intend to intrude upon my own essay. The editor and I thought that it might be interesting to relate some of the problems I have encountered (caused?) during my thirteen or so years of publishing. To wit, *The Outsider* above, had a dust wrapper illustration by Virgil Finlay, it being a collage of previously published illustrations rather than a painting done specifically for the book. With my first two books, though, I was smart enough to commission two fine artists to illustrate a scene from the books rather than the mishmash Arkham House got. Unfortunately, I was not smart enough to remember to typeset jacket copy for the dust wrapper flaps of the first book and was forced by a deadline to perfect-type the copy rather than typeset it, a glaring error that brightly outshines the Arkham House choice of a collage. Of course, I did not repeat this error with the second book's dust wrapper; I created a different one. While I remembered to give instructions for dust-wrapper flap copy and for spine copy on the book itself, I neglected them for the dust wrapper's spine. Of course, that spine copy is to aid in locating the book on a shelf and the book does stand out on a shelf by being the only book spine without print! Arkham House never did that!

While Arkham House is well known for books it published, it (as are many other specialty presses) is also known for books it announced and did not publish. Probably the best known is Manly Wade Wellman's *Worse Things Waiting* announced as forthcoming in the late 1940s. Unlike a lot of such books, it did see print although from Carcosa rather than Arkham House. The 1973 publication date was about a quarter-century late. Yes, late is another specialty of the specialty presses! I cannot tell you how many letters I get from customers asking (well, demanding may be a better choice of words) why a book is not ready as announced. I must admit that a great deal of the delays can be attributed to the lack of experience some of us have; however, it is as easy to fall under the rule of Murphy's Laws as the weight of our inexperience. A case in point was my press's *The Scallion Stone*. Now there is a strange story. Without delving into it too deeply, let me state that was a book containing the only five stories written by an author who never submitted them for publication during his lifetime. That is certainly not an auspicious start for a book from a nonprofessional press, but things went well up until the dust wrapper (my bugaboo, it seems). We specialty press people like to lean on each other for help, and I learned about a Taiwanese firm from Ted Dikty (FAX, Starmount) that did inexpensive but good color separations. I decided to try them out with *The Scallion Stone* cover and sent them the original art. I was given a turnaround time of three weeks. Four weeks later, the book was printed, but the color separations had not arrived. Five weeks. Six weeks. Seven weeks. I began to feel something was wrong and called them, but my phone call only made things worse. The painting had been stopped in customs about six weeks before and shipped back to me. I went to the post office, but it was "too soon" to send a tracer. Then my printer called me and was talking about charging me storage if I did not get him the art for the dust wrapper. By sheerest luck, my collecting mania had generated some original commissions by the same artist whose painting was lost. My crazed mind found a portion of one painting that actually fit one scene from a story in *The Scallion Stone*. I unframed the painting, sent it to a local color separator (at five times the cost), and had my cover. The story, though, does not end here. A couple of weeks later, during a snowstorm, a huge truck pulled up in front of my house. Of course, the truck contained three thousand pounds of *Scallion Stones* that the trucker would not unload due to his union contract. So I began dragging sixty or so cartons off his truck, up my driveway, and into my garage. When I was about halfway finished, the mailman pulled up and asked me to sign for a package. Here, nine weeks in arriving, was the original painting for *The Scallion Stone*. The circle was completed, but the story is not. Specialty-press people waste not, want not. Five years later when I was unable to get the cover art I wanted for my Doubleday anthology, *Whispers IV*, I was finally able to use *The Scallion Stone* art on a book jacket.

Arkham House's first book to prove a true financial success was A. E. van Vogt's *Slan* (over four thousand copies of this sold at a $2.50 list price). With this "huge" "best-seller," others saw the potential publishing value of science fiction books (most of Arkham House's titles to that time were horror- and fantasy-oriented). The first major specialty press to jump onto the train was Fantasy Press (not to be confused with Crawford's Fantasy Publishing Company, Incorporated [F.P.C.I.]), a group of people headed by author Lloyd Arthur Eshbach and—surprise!—their first volume was *The Book of Ptath* (1947) by *Slan*'s author, A. E. van Vogt. Over the more than fifteen years of their existence, Fantasy Press published first editions by E. E. Smith, John W. Campbell, Jr., Robert Heinlein, Jack Williamson, Stanley Weinbaum, Eric Frank Russell, L. Sprague de Camp, John Taine, Murray Leinster, and others. Some of their major titles included Weinbaum's *A Martian Odyssey and Others* (1949), Russell's *Sinister Barrier* (1948), Heinlein's *Beyond this Horizon* (1948), and E. E. Smith's famed Lensman series, The History of Civilization. A collecting oddity occurred with this series in that the Fantasy Press's reprinting of their own first editions of this grouping are worth much more than the true first editions. This was probably due to the fact that the reprinting was on better paper, specially signed, and had leather spines, but the real reason may be the strict limitation to only seventy-five, mostly prepaid, sets. Whatever the reason, it is close to being or may well be the fantasy and science-fiction specialty presses' most expensive item. I should note here that Fantasy Press was the first of the 1940s' specially presses to offer signed editions. Generally, the first 300–500 copies of each of their titles were inscribed or signed by the authors and, unlike most of today's signed editions, were sold prepublication and prepaid at the list price for the trade editions.

1947 saw the previously mentioned F.P.C.I. come into being and their first hardcover title was *Out of the Unknown* authored by, you guessed it, A. E. van Vogt. F.P.C.I. does not have the literary reputation of Arkham House or Fantasy Press or some of the later specialty publishers, and the collectibility of their books reflects that. Still, they published some decent work to include A. Reynold Morse's bibliographic *Works of M.P. Shiel* (1948), L. Ron Hubbard's *Death's Deputy* (1948), Olaf Stapledon's *World of Wonder* (1949), and L. Sprague de Camp's *The Undesired Princess* (1951). Other authors published by F.P.C.I. included John Taine, Murray Leinster, Ralph Milne Farley, and Stanley Weinbaum. F.P.C.I. stopped publishing in 1953.

While Arkham House has my vote for *the* specialty press, it always (until recently) leaned far more towards the horror-fantasy side of science fiction rather than the nuts-and-bolts area. My choice for *the* specialty press in the hard science fiction arena is the infamous Gnome Press. Founded in 1948 by Martin Greenberg (not to be confused with the noted anthologist Martin H. Greenberg) and David Kyle (who later left the enterprise), the stories have it that Greenberg was notoriously slow with payments, when they were made. And it is true the physical materials he used were not the best available, merely the most affordable (cheapest?). Putting those rather large black marks aside, though, we find a specialty press that originated major classics of science fiction and fantasy, including Asimov's Foundation Trilogy plus his *I, Robot* (1950), Judith Merrill's *The Year's Greatest Science Fiction and Fantasy* series, Clifford Simak's *City* (1952), C. L. Moore's *Shambleau and Others* (1953), Fritz Leiber's *Two Sought Adventure* (1957), and Robert E. Howard's original Conan books. And there were more books by these authors as well as some by Robert Heinlein, Arthur C. Clarke, Jack Williamson, Fred Pohl, and many others. It should also be noted that Greenberg himself edited several significant science-fiction anthologies for his press and that several Gnome Press originals were then and are still being reprinted by commercial publishers in both paperback and hardcover versions.

A fourth late-1940s' specialty press of note was Shasta Publishers. Shasta's existence was due to the efforts of Erle Korshak and Everett F. Bleiler, the company having been formed to print Bleiler's landmark bibliography, *The Checklist of Fantastic Literature* (1948; expanded, retitled, and revised in 1978 and published by Firebell Books). The press would have lived on in history had this been its only book, but they did much more. Highest on their honor roll must be the first three books in Robert Heinlein's Future History Series. These were *The Man Who Sold the Moon* (1950), *The Green Hills of Earth* (1951), and *Revolt in 2100* (1953). In addition to these, there were such notable titles as Alfred Bester's Hugo Award-winning *The Demolished Man* (1953), John Campbell's *Who Goes There* (1948), and Raymond Jones's *This Island Earth* (1952). Shasta ceased to exist in 1957. Finances played a part in this, but the most immediate reason given by many was the ill-will generated by their nonpayment to Phillip José Farmer of his prize money from a novel-writing contest. Interestingly enough, that novel formed the basis for Farmer's now-famous Riverworld Series and has earned for the author many thousands of dollars more than the contest's prize as well as winning him a Hugo Award. It is also a fact that other Shasta authors had financial "arguments" with Mr. Korshak so the Farmer incident was not an isolated one, merely the proverbial straw that broke the camel's back.

The fifth and last of the major 1940s' specialty presses was Prime Press, a venture formed by Oswald Train, Jim Williams, Bud Waldo, and .Alfred Prime. (I will let you guess who financed most of the venture.) They published some very attractive books to include works by Dr. David Keller, Lester del Rey, Nelson Bond, and L. Sprague de Camp; however, I feel their claim to fame was issuing Theodore Sturgeon's first hardcover book *Without Sorcery* (1948). This is a fine collection as well as being a sought-after collectible, especially in the eighty-eight-copy signed and slipcased edition. Still rarer, though, was the pre-publication state of part of the book, itself a "book." Titled *This Is "It,"* the twenty-nine-page pamphlet contained the complete story "It" as taken from *Without Sorcery*. Only fifty copies of this booklet were printed. The booklet was a promotional device for *Without Sorcery* and was sold at 1948's World Science Fiction Convention held in Toronto. Essentially, Prime Press died when Jim Williams passed away in 1951.

There were some other notable publishers during these postwar years to include The Buffalo Book Company; the Chamberlain Press, Incorporated; and Hadley Publishing Company. They did not, though, publish the quantities of books the others did. Most major of the Buffalo Book Company's two books was the classic E. E. Smith volume, *The Skylark of Space* (1946). The Chamberlain Press was only a one-shotter with Richard Matheson's well-known first book, *Born of Man and Woman* (1954). And Hadley's best were L. Ron Hubbard's *Final Blackout* (1948) and John Campbell's *The Mightiest Machine* (1947).

Speaking of *The Mightiest Machine*, I will again intrude with a tale. Don Grant, one of Hadley's founders, has dubbed me "The Variant Man." It was not, I think, due to my appearance, but rather to the fact that I tried to collect all the different states of a book. While engaging in this task with *The Mightiest Machine*, I noted that the two copies I had differed in their binding cloths. I asked Don about this and he related that there were at least half a dozen different cloths used to bind that title. Apparently it is a standard printing practice to give a less-expensive price to customers who allow the binder to choose the cloth and use up all his left-over stock on one particular book. It was a money saver for all concerned. This is a little bit different from the Greenberg variants of Fantasy Press titles and Greenberg's Gnome Press books, situations wherein the books were bound with the cheapest materials possible. It was a lot different from my Whispers Press's experience with Fritz Leiber's *Heroes and Horrors* (1978). I like the tactile sensations of a rough cloth on a book; it is a covering that feels like a book. In that regard, I have had all but two of my books bound in a high-grade buckram cloth. There is not much call for this cloth due to its higher price, but I wanted it. After much thought, I chose a coffee-brown buckram for *Heroes and Horrors*. During the binding process, I got a panic-filled call from my printer saying we had wiped out the cloth company's entire stock of the coffee-brown cloth, and it would be weeks or months before the company would be able to make more. I hit the selection book again and chose a maroon-colored cloth to fill out the run. A day or two later found me at the receiving end of another panic-filled call. We had done it again, no more maroon cloth. Finally, the beige cloth of my third choice proved sufficient in quantity to finish the run. The Whispers Press had done it. Rather than getting three different cloths at a bargain price, I paid full price for the privilege of using up the binder's remnants!

I have previously noted that the specialty presses grew due to the commercial publishers' reluctance to take a chance with fantasy and science fiction. I believe this is true. Yes, there were some efforts by the professionals in the early-to-mid 1940s (notably, Henry Holt and Company's three L. Sprague de Camp titles, Pocket Books's paperback edition of Donald Wollheim's *The Pocket Book of Science Fiction* [1943], Groff Conklin's Crown Publisher's edition of *The Best of Science Fiction* [1946], and the milestone anthology from Random House, Raymond Healey's and J. Francis McComas's *Adventures in Time and Space* [1946]), but until the late forties and early fifties, the fantasy and science-fiction publishing field was the playground of the fans and their speciality presses.

I feel the tables were turned by Scribner's publication of the now-famous Robert Heinlein "juveniles" such as *Rocket Ship Galileo* (1947), *Space Cadet* (1948), and *Red Planet* (1949). Then Doubleday Books began to pick up on science fiction. Their early lineup was absolutely mind-staggering. They had Asimov's *Pebble in the Sky* (1950), Ray Bradbury's *The Martian Chronicles* (1950), Robert Heinlein's *The Puppet Masters* (1951), Hal Clement's *Mission of Gravity* (1954) and much more. All of a sudden the writers who previously had only the speciality presses to turn to now had greener pastures.

And the greener pastures of the early fifties also included paperback publishers, most notably Ace Books and Ballantine books (who also did some of their books in short-run, and now collectible, hardcovers). Indeed, my own introduction to the science-fiction book world was through these paperbacks. Ace was noted for their special "doubles," two novels back to back, each with separate covers. And the Ballantine line was equally memorable with their surrealistic covers by the extremely talented Richard Powers. The list of paperback publishers grew and grew, and the science-fiction and fantasy magazines proliferated as well. It was the heyday of the field, except for the specialty presses which went into low gear or no gears at all.

Let me drop back here, for a moment, and explain why the specialty presses went into partial eclipse. The simple reason was competition. The professionals could market books better and pay more money. The more complex but just-as-true reason was the rationale for the specialty presses' existence, or any business's existence, in the first place, *need*. The need for the presses was no longer 100 per cent there. The presses had sprung up because there were people who wanted book editions of certain works and no professional publisher wanted to do them. Now the professionals saw a market they could exploit and they stepped into what the fan publishers had created. And they took that market away. Yes, Gnome Press and Fantasy Press survived into the late fifties and Derleth's Arkham House, anticipating the reduced need, slowed down, but for the most part, fantasy and science-fiction specialty publishing barely survived during the late fifties and early sixties. There was Mirage Press publishing a few titles, mostly nonfiction stuff that the professionals had no interest in, and there was Donald Grant, a partner in Hadley and other fan presses, publishing some nonfiction work as well as some Robert E. Howard fiction that was still considered unmarketable to mass audiences. That was it for then. Now, though, we are past the seventies and into the eighties and fantasy and science fiction specialty presses are once again springing up. Why?

The answer, of course, is still the same reason the presses originated in the first place, *need*. As time went by, it became obvious that there was a need for certain works in more attractive and better constructed packages than the professionals could cost-consciously produce. There also became a market for books specially signed and slipcased. And there still was a market for books the professionals considered too risky for mass market consumption. The fan publishers leaped into the breach.

At the top of the list in the sixties and still there in the eighties is Donald Grant. This fantastic man has produced incredible books, their directions being as varied as you can imagine. He has produced many collections of Robert E. Howard's stories and poetry, large volumes of artwork, impressive scholarly bio-bibliographies, illustrated novels, and more. Of special note among the many Grant books we find the Jeff Jones – illustrated editions of *Red Shadows*, Robert E. Howard's Solomon Kane stories; the Edgar Rice Burroughs bibliographic bible, *A Golden Anniversary Bibliography of Edgar Rice Burroughs* (1964); the illustrated Conan series; a collection of George Barr's color artwork, *Upon the Winds of Yesterday* (1976); and, most recently, impressive illustrated editions of Stephen King's *The Dark Tower: The Gunslinger* (1982) and *Christine* (1983).

Although Don Grant was one of the first on the Robert E. Howard bandwagon, he was far from alone when Howard's Conan character gained national fame. The seventies boomed with Howardiana to include everything from Grant's beautifully produced Conan reprints to this-publisher-and-that's booklet of the most minor Howard words, often crudely typed and offset-reproduced. I will not even begin to attempt a listing of any of these titles; they came so fast and furiously that a formal bibliography would be needed to track them all down (one, by the way, that Grant published and titled *The Last Celt*, 1976). In the late seventies and early eighties, the boom ceased and both publishers and speculators now have a lot of Howardiana in stock that not even the recent Conan movie and comics seem to be moving. It shows perfectly the problem of filling a need when a need no longer exists.

In the above paragraph, and despite my perpetrating *Rime Isle*'s dust-wrapper copy on the field, I intimate my disgust with the crudely done Howard items. Lest you think, though, that typesetting is the only way to go on a book, let me relate a horror story regarding my typesetting on Robert Bloch's *Psycho II*, a story that almost made me wish that I had typed out the entire book for camera-ready copy! I had read *Psycho II* twice during the buying and copy-editing stages. I enjoyed the book, but by my third reading at the galley stage, some of the joy had worn off. It was now a job. And a tough job—not due to that particular book, but because only one set of eyes proofing presages glaring errors due to familiarity with the text. One tends to read what one knows should be there as opposed to what is there. By the page-proof stage (reading number four),

I was becoming downright married to the text instead of merely familiar. I persevered because I knew this would be my last full reading; any reading at the next stage would only require my going specifically to the page that I had marked for a correction. So on this fifth stage, when I found an error I had (apparently) overlooked at the fourth reading, I thanked my lucky stars that it had been near a previous error or I would have missed it. Still, it was a glaring mistake and for no sane reason, I rechecked the page proofs to see if it was there. (Have you ever rechecked an alarm clock you knew had been set? That is the same reason I checked here.) The error, though, was not on the page proofs! Holy Lovecraft, this could not be. Still, there it was. I very tenderly reread a chapter of the book and found more such "impossible" mistakes. I called my typesetter to find out why. Apparently, there was a "brown out" while *Psycho II*'s computer tape was being run. Somehow this must have caused some changes on the magnetic tape, resulting in the errors. I ended up rereading the book two more times. Oh for the cold-type you could see rather than the invisible gremlins on magnetic tape! Maybe the thirties were better than the seventies and eighties!

While the sixties and seventies did not see much other than the publishers and materials already mentioned, a market developed in the late seventies and early eighties that the specialty presses jumped into: the signed-edition market. With science fiction and fantasy in general and signed books in particular increasing in value on the out-of-print markets, perspicacious publishers observed and treated the trend. Presses such as Underwood-Miller, Phantasia Press, and my own Whispers Press doctored the "disease." This is not to say that we were the only ones or that we only filled a need for signed books. What we have tried to do is make better books (sewn-signatures, sturdy cloth bindings, acid-free paper and the like) as well as signed ones. We also try to supply the permanence of hardcovers where only paperbacks have been before. I feel that we have succeeded in all these efforts. In fact, we have succeeded too well.

How do you succeed too well? As with science-fiction magazines in the 1950s and the Howardiana in the 1970s, the market appears to be reaching a saturation level. It seems that almost every book being published is also being done by a specialty press in some sort of signed edition. Regardless of the quality of the book, though, there is always going to be a point that the supply will outstrip the demand, and I have already seen some buyer resistance despite the books by key authors (King, Heinlein, Asimov, and the like) still selling out on a regular basis. And here is another aspect of "too well." The professional publishers are beginning to notice that the big-name authors' books can easily be sold in signed editions, so easily that they are beginning to do these editions themselves rather than contracting them out to small presses or allowing the authors to reserve the rights for specialty presses. The fan publishers once again developed the market and the professionals are taking away the meatiest part.

In summary, the mid-eighties' market for signed books from the specialty presses is darker than it was in the late seventies due to the glut of books and the interference of the professionals. There is, though, a future for these presses. What is it? I think it is a threefold one. Firstly, with regard to signed editions, the press runs can be made smaller, the editions more special. Secondly, I think there will always be a market for the fine presses, the booklets and books with carefully selected type faces printed on special papers with hand presses. (This art has been exemplified in our field for many years by Ron A. Squires. His publications of work by Ray Bradbury, Howard Phillips Lovecraft, Clark Ashton Smith, Fritz Leiber, and Robert E. Howard have long been coveted by collectors.) Thirdly, and most importantly, the future for the presses lies with the creation of books the professionals do not think there is a mass market for. For instance, my own Whispers Press produced Fritz Leiber's 1978 collection, *Heroes and Horrors* (which, by the way, was one of the first specialty-press books in a long time that generated a reprint sale to the professionals) and the Scream/Press presented Dennis Etchison's *The Dark Country* (1982). And Carcosa, a triumvirate composed of Karl Edward Wagner, David Drake, and Jim Groce, created mammoth collections such as Manly Wade Wellman's *Worse Things Waiting* (1973) and Hugh B. Cave's *Murgunstrumm and Others* (1977), that both won World Fantasy Awards as best collections of the year. Still, in the long run, things will always be the same. When the professionals see some money along the paths trailblazed by the fan press, they will jump in; however, I feel that the fans will be waiting with ideas, original and old, and begin the cycle anew. I guarantee it!

The truth is, I hadn't thought of Carter Scholz for the next essay at all. I desperately wanted a diatribe on the "ghetto-ization" of science fiction, which those of us in the field know full well exists. My original choices were Barry Malzberg and Harlan Ellison, both of whom are quite vocal on the subject as they publicly continue to "resign" from the field. But Barry had said all he needed to say in his emotionally wrenching book *Engines of the Night*, and I couldn't afford Harlan.

When Barry originally recommended Carter Scholz, I racked my brain, trying to remember who he was. I thought Carter had to be a little old man with a long career in the field, one long enough to be able to knowledgeably comment on the ghetto. But Carter is not a little old man. He was only twenty-three when he was nominated for the Hugo, Nebula, and Campbell Awards all in 1977 and he continued to write like a fiend, whenever he wasn't forced to earn a living. That I couldn't place him only shows up those aspects of the science fiction field he discusses here.

His short stories have appeared in numerous magazines and anthologies, and his novel, *Palimpsests*, has been published as an Ace Special. He earns his living at computer programming (which he despises), brews his own beer, has built a clavichord and a synthesizer, and is currently rooting out spearmint, bamboo, and nasturtiums so as to build a compost heap atop his collection of science-fiction paperbacks.

On the whole, he'd rather be a musician, and here's why. . . .

5
INSIDE THE GHETTO, AND OUT
CARTER SCHOLZ

The idea of science fiction as a ghetto, as a place where writers receive separate and highly unequal treatment, was publicized by Harlan Ellison in the mid-1960s. Some time after that, Ellison made it a condition of his contracts that the words "science fiction" never appear on his books.

It has not helped much. Bookstores and libraries still file his work in category, he is still much in evidence at science-fiction conventions, and the New York critics have still failed to lionize him.

I start with Ellison because he was the first writer I met. It was 1973. I was nineteen. I wanted to write. I was footloose and fevered then, and I drove all night to Dartmouth College, where I had friends, and where he would speak.

He spoke long and well. He said the ghetto walls were coming down. He described science fiction as a fair, shining land, open to all comers, liberal and warm. He implied that if Franz Kafka were alive, his work would be called science fiction. He implied welcome.

I applauded. I was passionate in support of the weird, the imaginative, the subversive. I was young. I took these fine words at face value. Afterwards, I collared Ellison, and asked him what I was to do. I had a story in my hands.

Naturally, he balked. He said, "If you want to write this stuff, you should apply to the Clarion Writer's Workshop. Deadline's April something, workshop starts first of July at Michigan State. Write Lenny Isaacs. I'll be there."

I wrote Lenny Isaacs and sent a story. I was accepted, and I went. I had been reading Joyce, Eliot, Kafka, and Beckett. What a shock was in store.

Out of almost thirty young writers, there were just four who had read Joyce, Eliot, Kafka, or Beckett. I was the only one who had cracked *Finnegans Wake* or read Beckett's great trilogy. Half were innocent of Hemingway and Faulkner. And I was not advantaged; my only exposure to "literature" had been high-school English, and I hated it. I found nothing to admire in Henry James's *The Americans*. I positively resented Robert Frost's snowy woods. So strongly did I reject this force-feeding that I refused to go to a liberal arts college, assuming it would be four more years of the same. Instead I went to art school. And it was there I came, by myself, to works I could use.

Of course I had read science fiction. I had liked a bit of it. I had liked Ellison, and Disch, and Malzberg, and Wilhelm, and Le Guin, and Silverberg, and Ballard. I had liked Sturgeon and Bradbury. And when I started to write I took them as models, because their writing seemed attainable. Joyce, Eliot, Kafka, and Beckett did not, not at age nineteen. That is how I came to meet Ellison, and to attend Clarion, and to become a "science fiction writer," to all my later woe.

It was at Clarion that I began to perceive that the ghetto walls were still up. Ghettos are typically domains of the exiled. Certainly I felt exiled. My art school had been across the street from Brown University, and I had friends there, and when I ventured to speak of my reading with them, I was embarrassed. I didn't have their vocabulary. But I felt equally exiled at Clarion. I saw that the others were bright, introverted, and devoted, like myself. But their devotions were not mine. There were no aspirant Kafkas, not even an aspirant Disch. These students had read and loved more science fiction that I imagined existed. Even the science-fiction writers I admired were considered peripheral. How, I wondered, could anyone read both Philip Dick and Thomas Disch, and think Dick the better writer? How could anyone read A. E. van Vogt at all? As at

Brown, there was a code here, a vocabularly which I did not possess. I could see no artistic point to inventing a new kind of robot or alien, or to designing whole star systems as a backdrop for operatic adventures. Yet that was the basic vocabulary of science fiction.

Robin Scott Wilson, the originator of the workshop, gave us a rough working definition of a story: a character is confronted with a crisis and is changed by it. I was bold enough to mention Beckett, though I already realized that Beckett was as out of place here as Borges might be at a mystery-writers' convention. But Robins rose to it, saying, "Very well. The character is changed, or fails to change." So I was placated. Conceivably the practical, nuts-and-bolts approach of the workshop could permit even highly specialized and individual works.

The point of the workshop was to turn fledglings into professionals, in six intense weeks. Inevitably, then, it focused on what would sell rather than what would endure. No other approach would have been feasible with beginners. Aesthetic discussion would have been debilitating.

But what is meant by "professional" is vexing. At age nineteen it seemed wholly desirable, and it is the best possible goad to a beginner. But by this focus, Clarion performed the same normative function as the field at large, failing to note that "what will sell" is mutable, that the market is not a constant, that it is no reliable guide to excellence, and neglecting to say that professionalism is only partly craft skill. True, a writer's first sale almost always marks an improvement in craft. But shortly things change; the professionalism that leads to continued sales—to a career—is unrelated to craft (more to personal contacts, speed of execution, and reliability of approach), and can tend to pollute the craft. The emphasis of craft in the service of sales, then, is a correct and practical picture of the genre; but it encourages normative practice over individual development, exactly as in medieval guilds. Under a patronage system, this emphasis can serve excellence; under a market system, it cannot.

But this is hindsight. I mention it just to show how the reality of the market affects attitudes and approaches throughout the genre. At the time, I learned some craft lessons, and went off to apply them. And I sold some stories. I found this remarkable. I did not think that I wrote very well. But I knew I was improving, and counted this period as apprenticeship.

I soon improved myself right out of the market. Between 1977 and 1981 most of my short fiction—over one hundred thousand words of it, higher in ambition and cleaner in craft than the stuff I had sold—went begging. In the litany of rejections one term was constant: "well-written." In time I came to think that this was the *reason* for rejection, and I am still not so sure that I was wrong.

Another common response to my work then was that it was "not science fiction." This proved the futilityof trying to define the term, for the only true definition was that it was what could be sold and published as science fiction at a given time—and so would change from year to year in an inconsistent manner. (Indeed, I *was* able to sell several of these stories in 1983, at least one to the same market that had turned it down as "not science fiction" in 1980.)

So my sense of exile was fairly complete. Of course, I was not alone. This period was a bad one for the field. The original anthologies, which had been my first home, were dead or ailing. *Star Wars* proved that science fiction could be big business if one aimed at the lowest common denominator. Publishers were being bought out by conglomerates. There was fear and a widespread retrenchment from ambition.

But one of the pleasant aspects of exile is a sense of exemption. When Robert Silverberg, Harlan Ellison, and Barry Malzberg announced their several retirements from science fiction in 1975, it had not occurred to me that whatever had forced them to that decision could affect me. I learned that I was not exempt. I learned that the commercial nature of science fiction puts a varying limit on ambition and technique, and I had passed it. What Silverberg, Malzberg, and Ellison decided, in their various ways, at greater length and cost, was that there is no point to passing the limit. No professional point.

What is most interesting about the hard lessons of this period is that those who suffered the most came readily to see it as their own fault. Damon Knight, whose long-lived *Orbit* series was the greatest single force in the American "New Wave," said in his last volume that he had set "the highest standards," but "I followed this trail too far." Silverberg said of his audience, "Something was wrong, either with my perceptions or with their degree of literary response. I still don't know which it was, but I no longer care. I've come to see my response to it as my own folly." Kate Wilhelm, who with Knight was responsible for what literary standards Clarion had, said: "People aren't interested in good prose, or beautiful language. I wonder sometimes if it isn't a mistake to nitpick and go after the prose flaws in students, or even in other writers. Maybe it's beside the point." Even Malzberg, who alone of the casualties wrote at some length about the collapse of his career, came finally to conclude that he had been a fool to expect otherwise.

That is, the professional response to a failure is, at least publicly, to blame the work, not the audience. The customer is always, ultimately, right. This is the bottom line that encloses the ghetto, pernicious because of the collusion of the writers themselves at keeping it in place. *Not* to take this line as an item of faith is professionally suicidal.

I came into the field by accident, because it happened that when I started to write experimentation was a viable commodity. When this changed, almost overnight, I was slow to catch on. In short, I learned that science fiction is in practice a commercial category, not a literary genre. Only at times, and incidentally, is literary ambition permitted.

In theory, I still believe otherwise.

Making a gross dichotomy, prose literature might be divided into two parts: the novel of manners, and the novel of ideas. These existed side by side into the twentieth century—at which time there was a certain falling-off in the novel of ideas. For the ground of ideas had shifted. Religion and philosophy were no longer the only major gardens of thought; fruitful ideas were now to be found in science, politics, and language itself.

USA, Darkness at Noon, Man's Fate, works by Solzhenitsyn and Böll are political novels of ideas. Joyce, Kafka, and Beckett are clearly writing in the realm of ideas of another sort. But what this has left largely untouched is ideas of modern science and technology. Aldous Huxley was perhaps the last major writer to have a grasp both of letters and scientific ideas. He went far enough in *Brave New World* to imply the intimate, complex, modern connection between science and politics. Thomas Pynchon would take it further in *Gravity's Rainbow*. There are a few novels of purely scientific ideas, such as Huxley's *After Many A Summer Dies the Swan*, or John Banville's recent *Kepler*. But considering how dominant science and technology have become in our lives, I find it remarkable that these ideas are so little touched.

Why is that so? First, the ideas are daunting. To subsume them in a literary work is not easy, and few writers have the vocabulary for it. Second, it has become thankless work. And here I detect the influence of the ghetto.

Except for some literary historians, "science fiction" did not start life by dealing with ideas. H. G. Wells's novels of ideas did not need a unique name when they were published. The term, and the modern genre, were invented by Hugo Gernsback in 1926. He published badly-written adventure stories with futuristic backdrops. His avowed intent was not literary; he meant to interest young boys in scientific careers. (Interestingly, John Campbell, whose aims were more literary, seems to have done a better job at this.) But Gernsback's influence on the genre to this day is undisputed. As late as 1953 it was decided to name the first science-fiction award after him.

This was the start of the ghetto: a separate term, and the initial unconcern with ideas. The writing improved markedly over the next few decades, but the genre still dealt in notions, not ideas. The assumption was that once you had your extrapolation and exposition in place, the job was half done, whereas that is really where the job starts. Critics took one look, and decided to ignore the field thenceforth. No work published in the ghetto, it seemed, could ever receive serious attention. As Damon Knight said, never had a genre been judged so exclusively by its worst examples.

And those writers outside the genre, who might have written novels of ideas of science—well, there was the example of the ghetto, a little enclave where people were writing earnestly and usually poorly about what they called science, where their work appeared between garish covers, was read mostly by adolescent boys, and got no serious notice. Under the circumstances, a man would have to be a fool or an impregnable Huxley to go anywhere near the territory. And if a man was fool enough to try, surely his agent or editor would warn him off.

Yet writers for whom the mores of suburbia were not all-engrossing did continue to go near these ideas. Kurt Vonnegut was one, and he was badly burned for it. His first book, *Player Piano*, was a novel of ideas about technology; but by 1953, the novel of ideas had withered to a point where publishers were uneasy with it. So the book was retitled and issued as science fiction, to Vonnegut's lasting chagrin. It is arguable that without science fiction Vonnegut would have had no audience at all, but he is understandably bitter that it took him nearly twenty years to be regarded as a serious writer.

The stigma is wearing off somewhat. More literary writers are coming to the ideas of science fiction now. Doris Lessing has devoted considerable effort to a multivolume space opera. Norman Mailer is reportedly at work on a long novel set in the future, on a spaceship. Bernard Malamud recently wrote a novel set after a nuclear war. And there are less well-known writers who seem more interested in the ideas than fearful of the stigma. I will return to this. In the meantime, what of life within the walls?

It must be understood that the readership of science fiction turns over almost completely every three or four years. These transient readers are mostly adolescents. That means that apart from a small core the audience has no historical sense of the genre, and small literary sophistication. Publishers respond to this by reissuing the same books, or the same kinds of books, over and over.

The vast majority of science-fiction writers are part of the core group. They have generally had a passionate adolescent involvement with the genre. They have also, as a rule, been precocious. First publication comes not uncommonly in the writer's teens. So, along with the commercial impetus to repeat one's successes, there is a premium on an adolescent world view. One is in a sense writing "best" when writing for the callow reader one once was.

The involvement with the audience is kept up by a social network that centers about conventions. Hardly a week passes in the US without a science-fiction convention somewhere, and writers are invited as the drawing cards. Editors and publishers attend; business is done; connections are made. The milieu of devotion and mutual admiration is like what I saw at Clarion: a group of exiles sharing and defending what they have in common. And what they have in common is science fiction, the whole gory indiscriminate history of it, from Gernsback on, and the emotional investment in that early reading, however bad it looks through mature eyes.

It is a warm atmosphere, but it has nothing to do with writing. It especially has nothing to do with writing past the established limits, for that would be a renunciation of the community, which defines itself by those limits. (The loyalty and sentiment offered are balanced by vicious backbiting and gossip, as in any ghetto. In the academic community, another sort of ghetto, the saying is: the infighting is so fierce because the stakes are so low.)

Writing is always an inhuman practice—Joan Didion says, "writers are always selling somebody out"—but nowhere so much as in this field, which has the aspect of an extended family, a family that one can never quite throw off, a family that is bound to praise or censure immoderately one's least strivings. Where is the writer who never resented his family? And what a nightmare this enormous, raucous family, so sensitive to betrayal, can be!

In addition to overpraising or undervaluing its members, the family is defensive against outsiders. In 1973, at the last gasp of the "New Wave," *Gravity's Rainbow* reached the final ballot of the Nebula award. It was soundly defeated by Arthur C. Clarke's *Rendezvous With Rama*. Despite the understandable sentiment toward Clarke, despite Pynchon's probable disdain of the award, despite the shortcomings of *Gravity's Rainbow*, it is clearly the better novel. *Rendezvous* is no novel at all, more a schematic diagram in prose. And mark you, the Nebulas are voted by the writers, not the fans.

The obvious message, given not for the first time, was that no work from outside could win a ghetto award. Vonnegut, by renouncing his connections with the ghetto, put himself beyond the pale. Ray Bradbury likewise, simply by shifting his work from the pulp markets to the slick magazines, was effectively denied any recognition from the ghetto, although he was the first of the ghetto writers to impress outside critics with his genre work—a fact which was probably more important to the genre's health than the complete works of Asimov.

The closure seemed complete. Each side of the wall would ignore the other.

If the ghetto is so restrictive, why not get out? The answer is at once true and self-serving: it is not so easy.

Theodore Sturgeon once offered a literary novel to his publishers; they would not publish it under his name. Robert Silverberg published a historical novel in 1983; *Publishers Weekly* reviewed it in their science-fiction department. My own efforts to find an agent have been thwarted by my refusal to write a second science-fiction novel; the task would be easier had I never published anything. There are many, many examples. Publishers, editors, agents, and readers are comfortable with categories, with success however modest, and trying something new can make the writer very uncomfortable.

So it is easier to stay in. The minimum standards for publication are low, and once you are published it becomes a habit to be published. There can be almost physical pain at spending your time and effort on something that will prove unwanted. There is a strong impetus not to write what you suspect your proven markets will be closed to. No writer, I suspect, is immune to the authority of publication, however debased the grounds of authority may be; even Kafka wanted all his unpublished work destroyed at his death, thinking it inferior.

So the state of the market can become self-enforcing, as writers cease to write the immediately unsalable. Outside markets are less receptive still. And quite likely there is a Norse fear of being outcast from a community of outcasts, for *that* exile is almost surely death.

Still, the walls would give a bit. During the ten years of the Vietnam war, two things happened in science fiction: the market expanded, and some universities offered courses in the genre.

This expansion was fueled by the demographics of the baby boom and a wartime economy. A new, large generation, educated in the math-and-science-oriented high schools of the post-Sputnik era, was reaching the ideal age for science-fiction readership. The political climate was one of dissent. The cultural climate was one of experimentation. More and various markets sprang up. Without this chance confluence, there would have been no "New Wave," not in America at least, but the happenstance was heady stuff. Out of the ghetto! The pay was still miserable, reviews benighted, the internecine strife of the family intolerable (one half yelling for progress! the other half whimpering for the return of Gernsback), but there was a feeling of freedom.

It didn't last. When the war ended, the economy retracted, and so did the field. The new audience had of course grown up and gone away. The writers, after a period of shock, retrenched. Silverberg, after the cold precisions of *Dying Inside* and *The Book of Skulls*, went to the gassy dreamscapes of *Lord Valentine's Castle*, et seq. Disch, after the masteries of *Camp Concentration* and *334*, turned to the kitsch of *On Wings of Song*. Even J. G. Ballard, the dour Briton who had produced *The Atrocity Exhibition* and *Crash!*, came back with the gentle, Bradburian *The Unlimited Dream Company*. And the retrenchment down in the ranks was more marked. All of which proved either amazing coincidence or just how closely the genre's literary aspirations were tied to the state of the market.

However, the academic interest, not being tied to the market, went on.

There had been criticism before, but it had come from within the field. The key works were Damon Knight's *In Search of Wonder* and James Blish's *The Issue at Hand*. Acerbic and prescriptive, these works set out to kill a lot of the clumsiness and bad writing endemic to the genre, and they succeeded. Their credos were straightforward. Blish: "The writing of science fiction is an activity which cannot usefully be divorced by the critic from the mainstream of fiction writing." Knight: "Ordinary critical standards can be meaningfully applied to science fiction." Yet even they (Knight more so than Blish) succumbed to overpraise, a kind of selective blindness amounting almost to apology in some cases.

Curiously, the obvious shortcomings of the genre were not shown up in the presumably harsher light of the academy. Rather, the apologia became more elaborate. Some went to tortuous extremes of semiotic analysis and Marxist exegesis to lend luster to the object of their study. Some put forth the theory, directly counter to Knight and Blish, that science fiction *cannot* be judged by normal criteria; that literary skill is somehow irrelevant, or even inimical, to the genre.

The point has some validity, for science fiction has become a specialized languge. Samuel Delany observes that some intelligent readers simply cannot make sense of it, because they are unfamiliar with the vocabulary and concepts built up through the history of the field—and the writers are often at no pains to make them accessible.

But by accepting this historically conditioned state of affairs as given and correct, the academy makes science fiction ever more specialized and self-referring. It reinforces the commercial boundaries without acknowledging their existence. More grievously it tells us nothing useful about the place of science fiction as literature, only about science fiction as science fiction.

This approach, I think, is wrong—or at least incomplete. As Ezra Pound said, you cannot learn anything about a substance by comparing it to more of itself.

There are good reasons to make comparative studies within the genre, and to trace developments through major works. It would doubtless be instructive to study *why* some important book is badly written. The standard practice of selling a book before it is written, for instance, has surely determined the evolution of the field—but you would never know that the practice exists from reading most criticism. (Barry Malzberg's

Engines of the Night is the first full-length study to address this, and for that reason alone it is significant; it has other riches besides. See also Algis Budrys's chapbook *Nonliterary Influences on Science Fiction*.) But ultimately this work is literary history. For criticism one needs a broader view.

Fredric Jameson, a Marxist critic who occasionally writes on science fiction, and whose latest book, *The Political Unconscious*, is a study of literary genres, may be closest to the approach that would consider commerce, genre, and the larger literature in right proportion. But he has not so far produced an extended argument.

Except for lists of precursors in the novel of ideas, I have seen only fitful attempts to link the genre with any larger tradition. I have seen no attempts to connect it with other literature of its time. I have not seen it proposed that science fiction may be a transitional stage from the old novel of ideas to a new novel of ideas.

I think this last possibility is the genre's best hope.

Let us restate our earlier dichotomy. Say that literature is divided into the mundane and the imaginative.

The mundane is of this world. It describes the day to day of the here and now. It accords in all significant details to what we agree upon as temporal reality.

A work of imaginative literature is one in which the author *must* provide some exposition of his working reality, because it differs in a significant way from common reality.

This is not meant to be a definition of science fiction, or simply a new improved term to cover the same ground, like Heinlein's "speculative fiction." But science fiction can be subsumed wholly within this definition. More important, the definition lets in a range of other works, and points to what science fiction has in common with other literary tradition.

The definitions would include *Robinson Crusoe* and *Gulliver's Travels*. (The common concerns with exploration and scientific method are patent.) It could include some historical novels. (By and large, exposition here is provided as a convenience, not a necessity, since the facts are agreed upon, if not widely known. But on occasion, as with Banville's *Kepler*, exposition is necessary as well as convenient, to articulate connections between sets of ideas. This is also the case with *Gravity's Rainbow*.)

Finnegans Wake would be included, and the works of Borges, Kafka,

Bruno Schulz, some John Barth, perhaps John Hawkes. Works of surrealism are included.

At the margin, *Moby Dick, Heart of Darkness*, some works by Faulkner and "magic realists" (Marquez, Fuentes) might be let in. The worlds are "real," but intensely reimagined, as skewed from common reality as Kafka's Prague.

For a long time I have felt that works like these have affinities with the best concerns of science fiction. I think that the defining point of "necessary exposition" provides a working rule to test the congruence of concerns.

Not all science-fiction writers, but the majority, have looked largely to the genre itself for inspiration, techniques, underpinnings, and standards. This has kept the genre at a remove from general literature, and from a serious ongoing readership. It has remained first and foremost a market category, and attempts to breach this barrier from within have so far been futile, abortive, or exceptional.

Here are some exceptions. Stanislaw Lem has been published by *The New Yorker* and reviewed on the front page of *The New York Times Book Review*; but Lem's membership in the Science Fiction Writers of America was revoked when he published an article criticizing the banal aspects of science fiction. Thomas Disch has had some attention from outside the genre; but his best books, *334* and *Camp Concentration*, are at this writing out of print in America. Ursula Le Guin won a National Book Award for the last volume of her *Earthsea* trilogy; but it was given for "children's literature."

So far, there has not been a single writer of science fiction who has gained decisive recognition both within and without the genre.

My position is this: The subjects and themes of science fiction are the stuff of major literature, ever the more so as humanistic thought catches up with the scientific and technical progress of the century. "Science fiction" is a transitional stage between the old novel of ideas and a new novel of ideas informed by this progress.

The present commercial constitution of the field does not readily allow major literary efforts. More, attitudes within the field tend to reinforce the commercial status quo. The category is in no danger of dying as a commercial enterprise; but the genre stands increasingly in danger of having its tenuous claims to legitimacy usurped by a growing general interest in the imaginative treatment of ideas, especially scientific ideas.

Increasingly, writers who have a broader tradition than what is customary in the category are attacking these ideas, from a broad perspective and with good results.

So the question is whether "science fiction" writers, who almost alone and against the grain of their commercial situation kept the literature of ideas alive through the mid-century, will cling to their acquired label and their varying commercial security, or if they will recognize as kin the concerns of what I have called "imaginative literature." I think this reduces to either continuing in the defensive posture of the ghetto, or participating in the resurgence of a major literature form.

Speak of commercial restraints, critical lassitude, low advances, ignorant readers, purblind editors—all undeniably true. But as Barry Malzberg put it, "The real enemy is closer to home, and sometimes mutters in his sleep."

Some Recent Works
of Imaginative Literature

John Calvin Batchelor. *The Birth of the People's Republic of Antarctica.*
Samuel Beckett. *Endgame. Three Novels (Molloy, Malone Dies, The Unnameable). The Lost Ones.*
William S. Burroughs. *Nova. Naked Lunch. Cities of the Red Night. The Place of Dead Roads.*
Italo Calvino. *Invisible Cities.*
Guy Davenport. *Tatlin! Da Vinci's Bicycle.*
Don DeLillo. *Ratner's Star.*
William Gaddis. *JR.*
Russell Hoban. *The Lion of Boaz-Jochim and Jochim-Boaz. Kleinzeit. Riddley Walker. Pilgermann.*
Harry Mathews. *The Sinking of the Odradek Stadium and Other Novels.*
Vladimir Nabokov. *Ada.*
Flann O'Brien. *The Third Policeman. The Dalkey Archive.*
William S. Wilson. *Why I Don't Write Like Franz Kafka. Birthplace.*

One day I needed a new life. It was the same day of the annual Meet-the-Writers-and-Publishers gathering, sponsored by the Science Fiction Writers in America. I went to the gathering wearing a full-color sign specially made for me by the art department. It said: FOR SALE, ONE EDITOR.

Being that this was a gathering of creative, intelligent people, I expected all sorts of clever repartee. Well, the replies were less than brilliant, but I did get a very interesting offer: Marion Zimmer Bradley offered to trade lives with me. . . .

I actually considered it. Being known as the famous author of the Darkover books *was* appealing. I decided against it, but the encounter showed me yet another side to this unusual woman.

Marion Zimmer Bradley began writing in the 1950s, when she married and moved to Texas from New York, where she grew up on a farm. She wrote for "fanzines" (a term that is a combination of "fan" and "magazine"), and even published a fanzine of her own. But she admits to being terrible with numbers, and sometimes her fanzine would be labeled "either #23 or #24."

It was her "practice" writing for these fanzines that led to professional sales. She is most known for her many Darkover novels, currently published by DAW Books. Marion is unsure just how many Darkover books are in print; she hasn't counted them lately and thinks there are about eighteen. The Darkover novels are considered science fiction, though they have elements of fantasy. Darkover is an alien planet populated by a strange ethereal race, humans, and hybrids; descendants of Darkover often have psi powers. Marion also has a best-selling fantasy novel, *The Mists of Avalon*, and is currently working on several books, including a sequel to her Darkover novel, *Shattered Chain*.

Marion Zimmer Bradley look like someone's mother: she has short hair, a matronly figure, glasses. And she's often mothered troubled teenagers while doing psychological counseling and volunteer work. In fact, she's close to being a certified psychologist, but that's not likely to happen. After she began taking "all her clients' problems home and lying awake nights worrying about them," she decided to confine the problems to her literary characters.

It is her interest in people, I think, which explains her close and lasting ties to fandom. Not only has Marion come up through the ranks of fandom, but her Darkover novels have spawned a cult following. Many authors have a love/hate relationship with their readers, but Marion acknowledges her debt to fandom in this revealing essay. . . .

6

FANDOM: ITS VALUE TO THE PROFESSIONAL

MARION ZIMMER BRADLEY

I have a great deal in common with such science-fiction "greats" as Harlan Ellison, Isaac Asimov, Ray Bradbury, Robert Silverberg and Donald Wollheim—and others too numerous to mention: I came up through the ranks of fandom to become a pro writer. My first works, like theirs, were published in the letter columns of the old pulp magazines; later, in the pages of hectographed or mimeographed fanzines published by other young science fiction or fantasy fiction enthusiasts. Many of these fans, like myself, aspired to be professionals, and many of them actually made it; those I have mentioned, and many more. So many of these science-fiction and fantasy professionals came from the ranks of fandom, back in the days when science fiction was still a rather minor genre, that I once lightheartedly quipped that reading the 1965 membership list of the Science Fiction Writers of America (SFWA) was like reading the 1955 membership list of the Fantasy Amateur Press Association (FAPA).

That's not nearly as true as it used to be. In the years since 1966 or so, more and more writers are entering the ranks of science fiction and fantasy who have never had anything to do with fandom, and who tend, in fact, to be a little scornful of organized fandom, even when they attend its conventions and accept its awards. Writers such as Samuel R.

Delany, Ursula Le Guin, and Joanna Russ, clinging to their intellectual credentials from academia, are often gracious to fans when they must interact with them, but they do not, as do I and most of the others mentioned above, recognize their origins in fandom; and such writers as Gene Wolfe and Stephen King, while they may use fandom for publicity purposes, are occasionally snide or sarcastic about it. Fewer and fewer fans aspire to become professionals in any field—or if they do, it is harder to get in touch with their fellows.

Partly this is a matter of sheer *size*. When science fiction and fantasy were lumped together in the forties or thereabouts, there were, it was estimated, fewer than three hundred active fans who formed a loosely connected network of enthusiasts. There were fewer than half a dozen magazines published, and most of them had letter columns in the back pages, where potentially active fans could find the names and addresses of other fans, and could write to them and swap letters, friendship, and their own little magazines or fanzines. Many book collectors claimed that they bought literally everything published in either fantasy or science fiction in a given year—and could still do it without being millionaires, on the modest salaries of postal clerks or shoe salesmen.

I published my first fanzine on a pan hectograph which cost me five dollars, paying a dollar for a ream of paper, thirty cents for a special hectograph ribbon, and about a dollar for thirty three-cent stamps to mail it out with; and I joined in the cry of rage when paperback books went up to thirty-five cents, certain that no one would ever pay that much for them. (Just to keep perspective, a stamp is now twenty cents, paper is about ten dollars a ream, and my latest novel is advertised to sell at $3.50. The newest Montgomery Ward catalogue doesn't even advertise hectographs for sale anymore, and the cheapest mimeograph I've seen is about three hundred dollars instead of the $21.95 model I bought way back when. But then, the minimum wage has risen from fifty cents an hour to about $3.65. And wages have gone up to about six or seven times what they were then, but the price of publishing supplies, etc., has risen nearly ten times. Even with so-called teenage affluence, it costs more for the young enthusiast to start a fanzine, while the pulps, with their ready lists of names and addresses of fellow fans and other fanzines, are gone forever.)

Science fiction, of course, is now more respectable. It's easier to find other fans, the reader is not so isolated. Probably half of your graduating class has read Tolkien, Ursula Le Guin, Anne McCaffrey, and the latest

Heinlein or Frank Herbert. They have watched *Star Trek* on television, played Dungeons and Dragons or some science-fiction video game, stood in line to see the latest Lucas *Star Wars* epic or Steven Spielberg saga, and watched the moonshots and the space shuttle takeoff.

But this kind of fandom is not what it used to be—a refuge for young people who love *reading* above all things, a very specialized form of reading which isolates them from the other interests of the young people they know. Early fans were readers, compulsive readers of their chosen fiction, and often compulsive writers who, when they wanted to go and write the kind of thing they loved, couldn't get it published in their high-school magazine or college creative writing class without getting a lecture about wasting their good minds of trash. Or maybe even get hustled off to a school counselor to be brainwashed into taking more interest in what they called "healthy" reading: *Sports Illustrated* or *Good Housekeeping*, depending on your sex.

In those days, if you liked science fiction, there was no government space program, no NASA, no L-5 societies grabbing headlines, to reassure you that your interest in space was normal or even praiseworthy. A poll taken in 1952 or thereabouts showed no fewer than 10 percent of the public believed we would ever get to the moon, and of that 10 percent, almost none believed it would be before the year 2000. If you liked fantasy or horror you were even worse off. In the movies it was either Dracula or Disney, and psychologists were talking about how unhealthy it was to have any interest even in fairy tales. "Magical thinking" was the nasty epithet applied to anyone who was not completely materialistic. Nowadays about half of best-selling novels and more than half of popular movies have some supernatural or horror element; but back then anything to do with fantasy was rare and difficult to find.

So, in those days, when you met another fan, you were instant friends—even instant family in many cases. Behind all the rather childish feudin' and fussin', the immature name-calling in fanzines and silly teapot tempests, there was a very strong sense of togetherness. You were a member of a minority, and it created strong bonds. Even if you were, for instance, a devotee of *Weird Tales*, and the fan who lived across the city in the next town was dedicated to joining Rocket Societies and wanted to work in Space Technology, you were still under the blanket umbrella of fandom. You knew at least some of the same people. The two of you could talk without the ghastly left-out sense you felt at school, or at work, when it seemed the only subjects of mundane conversation were (for women) hair styles, fashions and dates for the Senior Prom, or (for young men) cars, baseball and girls.

Fandom, of course, still remains as a support group. It goes even further; at the last World Science Fiction Convention there were, I think, eight thousand fans, all of whom had at least *something* in common—they all cared enough about *some* aspect of the convention to buy a ticket and come to the hotel. That's very reassuring. Of course, there were a lot of them who also were interested in such peripheral fannish items as comic books, *Star Wars* games or Dungeons and Dragons game pieces, horror films, video games, L-5 colonies, or the Society for Creative Anachronism, costumes and the masquerade . . . you name it. There is still a hard core of fans interested in science-fiction writing, and in professional aspirations; but you can no longer walk up to any fan at a convention and assume that he or she shares your desire to work professionally in the field. Even if she wants to turn pro some day, she just might want to work as a lights technician for George Lucas instead of selling a story to *Analog*.

Many writers now, even those who came up through fandom, have very little to do with fandom as such. There is, for instance, a great difference, or so it seems to me, between the people who came into fandom through *Star Trek* and those who came in back in the days of the old pulps.

There is at least some good reason to think that it was *Star Trek* that made the difference. Those of us who were old-time fans and still dearly loved the television program quickly found out that *Star Trek* fandom was quite different from ordinary fandom. In 1962, for instance, when the Big Names were people like Isaac Asimov, Leigh Brackett, Ed Hamilton, Robert Heinlein, Poul Anderson, and Tony Boucher, a young writer just up from fandom could (as I did) get invited to a party in Chicago where all these living idols were sitting together in a single room and were willing to talk to you informally as a fellow writer or just as a human being who shared interests in common. You could sit on the same sofa, share a drink, and chat casually with these people, with no sense that there was a Great Fixed Gulf between you and the object of your interest. There was little, if any, sense that he was a Great Big Important Superstar and that you were a member of the Great Unwashed from whom the Star must be protected. Granted, even then there were teenage fans who made nuisances of themselves, demanded to tell the Big Names the details of their unwritten novels or the stories of their lives, and it became a rather rueful joke that some of the pro writers would hang out down in the bar (where teenagers, of course, would not be admitted) to get away from the more wearying and juvenile of their admirers.

But even the "down in the bar" attitude of some of the writers was a very far cry from the way gulfs were fixed between *Star Trek* Big Names and their fans. Granted that it is easier for thirty writers to relate to two hundred or even five hundred fans than for five or six film actors to relate to twenty thousand fans. But whatever the good reasons for the security surrounding the film and TV actors, it is *different*. The seventeen-year-old fan who had a chance for ten minutes of conversation, as I did with Leo Margulies and Sam Merwin, in 1947, could literally have her life changed. One does not reach that kind of metamorphosis by listening to a TV star or lining up for his or her autograph. I was deeply moved and inspired when I heard Mark Lenard of *Star Trek* speak, and I am sure that the appearances, and the role models presented by Nichelle Nichols and Grace Lee Whitney—to say nothing of Nimoy and Shatner—have raised the self-awareness and even perhaps the creativity of the fans who heard them. But it is a *different* inspiration. Only the tiniest minority, and then mostly those few who were working in security or guest liaison, ever had the opportunity to get to know these people as human beings like themselves, or to feel that what these people had done maybe they themselves could do. Many *Star Trek* fans, accustomed to meeting their celebrities only along the roped-off barricades of a thousand-person-long autograph line, were surprised and delighted when they found that a writer such as Poul Anderson or myself was a person who would sit and drink soda pop or beer and answer casual questions about their work in a casual way.

Please understand that I am in no way criticizing the celebrities of *Star Trek*, who with a few exceptions have been wonderful, charming people, making themselves accessible to their fans far above and beyond the call of duty; and despite all the unkind things people can and do say about actors, they too, like writers, are only human and mostly well-meaning. Whenever they dare to relax the façade of wariness (and having once been literally mobbed by fans at a huge convention, to the point where I feared for my physical safety, no one can blame, say, Leonard

Nimoy for his caution in venturing unescorted on to a hotel floor), they are wonderful people. Once when I appeared as guest writer at a convention where Grace Whitney ("Yeoman Rand") was the *Star Trek* guest, she and I enjoyed a couple of hours of very pleasant coversation. And I remember with great affection an episode where George Takei. ("Sulu") expressed interest in meeting A. E. van Vogt; I sat by, deeply moved and charmed by the interplay of mutual admiration and courtesy between the older writer and the younger actor. But there are so many *more* of their fans that they simply cannot get to know each and every one of them on a personal basis; while in the smaller and more intimate old-time fandom, based on books and magazines before the expansion of science fiction (in a larger sense) into the media, there was always a chance that any fan could meet, and get to know, almost any writer. That situation simply does not exist any longer and there is no way to bring it back. Even at science-fiction conventions, Robert Heinlein has had to show a certain caution in going out on the floor without someone to protect him against the well-meaning but almost dangerous adoration of his fans.

This being so, the question naturally arises as to whether fandom still has any uses for the writer and the would-be writer. Granted, science-fiction fandom—whether the fan is interested in standing in line to see yet another *Star Wars* epic, or in collecting different Dungeons and Dragons game pieces—is a wonderful hobby on any level. Collectors of comic books share the same kind of cameraderie as, say, Bela Lugosi fans. Those fans interested in "filk singing" gather in hotel rooms, lobbies and late-night party rooms to the point where the tone-deaf or the serious musicians have been known to protest that filk-singing, like sex, should be done in private by consenting adults. A word about "filk singing," actually, "folk singing"—but ever since a printing error in a program book, fandom adopted this new term. Where once there were two or three fantasy-oriented amateur press associations (apas) there now must be twenty or thirty, including one for Women's Studies, one for gays and lesbians, one for pagans, one for psychedelic experimenters, several for *Star Trek* and *Star Wars* fans, one highlighting pornography, and one for almost every big-city science fiction club . . . as well as probably a dozen others I don't even know about!

There are fanzines which run all the way from the two-page "personal-letter-mimeographed-for-a-few-close-friends" in the various apas, to highly professional fiction magazines with two-color covers and printed literary journals of serious criticism, many of which pay for material accepted and consider themselves all but prozines (magazines for professionals). There is no longer even a common base of assumed interest among all fanzine lovers or even all fanzine editors; the readers of an L-5 Society Newsletter cannot be automatically assumed to have anything in common with a fanzine of *Star Trek* amateur fiction. But almost every lover of the larger field which now takes in science fiction—not only printed books and magazines, but all the media—can find some recreational interest within the field, be his interest serious or frivolous.

Science fiction is one field where writers have always been able to get feedback. From the days of the old pulps—whose letter columns, unlike those written to, say, Western magazines, were filled with highly articulate commentary both from a scientific and a literary standpoint—science-fiction writers in general have known that they ignore the fans at their peril. Those writers who have never themselves been fans have been rather bemused by and occasionally resentful of this phenomenon. Some love it; some hate it; others shrug and matter-of-factly accept it as a godsend for publicity purposes. Some old-time fans have come very far from their origins and honestly don't like being reminded of them, such as Bob Silverberg. Some have turned on fandom; Harlan Ellison, especially, is given to caustic outbursts. Pragmatically, producers of *Star Trek* and *Star Wars* and such things have welcomed the active publicity among their fans; everybody knows the story of the writing campaign, kicked off by Bjo Trimble, which kept *Star Trek* alive for an extra season. Other writers, like myself, retain close sentimental ties with fandom and keep their connection with it very much alive. Jacqueline Lichtenberg and Katherine Kurtz, as well as myself, have found something very like a small cult fandom organizing around their work; I can't speak for any of the others (though I know that Anne McCaffrey, at least, has very mixed feelings about the desperate and often-articulated desire for her fans to *participate* in the Dragon/Pern universe by dressing in their clothes, speaking the language, writing amateur fiction).

Apart from the perfectly obvious benefits to sales—and before anything else, we must acknowledge that the Dorsai filksongs and fandom certainly benefit Gordon Dickson, that the Darkover fanzines create a ready-made market for new books for DAW, that Jacqueline Lichtenberg's crew of Sime/Gen fans and their fanzines probably play a part when an editor decides whether or not a new book will be bought—does organized fandom really have anything to offer the would-be professional writer?

At this point I could be accused of setting up a straw man, for a quick and pat answer, which says, Oh, yes, fandom is invaluable, that is established, it deserves absolute support, a writer can hardly do better than getting into fandom. If this were my only point, I could single out writer Susan Schwartz, who made her first bow in Darkover fandom, such artists as Alicia Austin and Hannah Shapero and George Barr, who made their reputations illustrating fanzines until they began to sell professionally, and point out the obvious, that such fanzines as *Algol* and *Fantasiae* and *Shayol* serve as training grounds for writing and editorial skills. Fandom has certainly proved its worth; not only the "old" style of fandom, producing greats in the field such as those I listed in the first paragraph, but the "new" style of fandom has supported the rise of many professional talents.

If it were only for this, fandom would have, I think, definitely established its worth. But there are, after all, other roads into professional accomplishment. Harlan Ellison, in one of his speeches, has attacked fandom for attempting to stereotype any writer as forever after somehow "belonging" to them, as if the writer had a duty to continue to write what his fans wanted. This is one of the very real dangers, and must be respected. The fact that I have chosen to remain attached to fandom as a part of my "roots" does not imply that Harlan must consider himself bound in honor to do the same; and there is something to be said for an attitude of total indifference to one's admirers, especially where the alternative is to remain bound by their wishes and desires. I have been pressed often to write sequels to certain books and I admit I have sometimes wondered whether I have been pressured to write books which perhaps should have remained unwritten, out of a desire for the security of a guaranteed following and assured popularity at least among my own personal fandom. I suppose this can be said of everyone who writes a series, from the followers of Darkover to the followers of Lord Peter Wimsey or Travis McGee. There is a telling passage in one of Louisa May Alcott's books where the writer Jo speaks of the insatiable demands of her fans and the desire at the end of *Jo's Boys* where the author speaks of the temptation to conclude her books with an earthquake which will sink Plumfield to the depths of the earth so that she could never be tempted to resurrect those characters and scenes. Conan Doyle threw Sherlock Holmes over the Reichenbach Falls, but was forced to resurrect him.

This is not to say that the Darkover books I have written by what I choose to call popular demand are worse books than any of the ones I wrote, and keep writing, to please myself. The demand of my personal public and my personal fandom, which can become very demanding indeed, has required me to go into new areas which have been previously unexplored. It is true that I occasionally wonder whether, if I had not been bound to Darkover by sentimental ties and a very real desire to please my fans, what else I might have been writing which might have been better. But when I get to worrying about that, I also remind myself that Sir Arthur Sullivan despised, or affected to despise, the wonderful light operas he wrote in collaboration with W. S. Gilbert, (which alone gave him his fame) and believed that his "true reputation" would rest upon such ponderous pieces of Victorian schlock as his cantata "The Golden Legend" and his opera *Ivanhoe*, both of which, with his other floods of pious twaddle, have found a well-deserved obscurity alongside the "serious historical novels" of Conan Doyle . . . the books he felt he should have followed with others after he ceased to write of the immortal Sherlock. There is usually a good reason for the popularity of certain types of fiction.

Fandom, then, at least for the writer who has achieved this kind of cult following, has some distinct uses for the writer. The floods of *Star Trek* fiction have encouraged such writers as Jacqueline Lichtenberg, Jean Lorrah, Ruth Berman, Shirley Maiewski, to reach for the professional milieu.

But it can be argued that the Lichtenbergs and Lorrahs, the Susan Shwartzes and Diana Paxsons, would have achieved fame and professional status in any case; talent will out. In the absence of Darkover, *Star Trek*, Deryni or Pern fandom and fiction writing, would not these writers have found some other way into the desired professional status? Did not these fandom-style endeavors rather divert and delay these writers from the undivided pursuit of their professional goals?

That is not such a simplistic question as it may sound. Even in the relatively simpler climate of fandom in the fifties, there came a time when I realized I was spending so much time on fan writing, fan publishing, and fan correspondence that I had no time for getting writing done and offering it for sale. In 1953 I made a relatively simple vow to cut back my fan activity and finish up a minimum of one story a month till I sold something; it was that year that I sold my first big novelette to the *Magazine of Fantasy and Science Fiction* and entered the ranks of pro writers. In 1963

I once again became so involved in the work of a little apa called *Apa X* that I had to make a distinct effort to gafiate (a fannish term for getting away from it all—"it all" meaning frantic fan activity) and get back to writing again. And just recently I have discovered that the level of fan publishing I have been doing in Darkover fandom has been draining energy I need for my professional work and commitments, and so I have dissolved my personal involvement with Darkover fanzine publishing.

So; without this involvement in fandom, would my professional life have been more productive, or more quickly remunerative? I don't know. It's possible. But then, even as it is, I am a high-output writer; I doubt if I could have done much more writing than I *have done* over these years. All the time of my fannish involvement, I have been turning out two or three books a year (including one or two blockbusters of more than two hundred thousand words) in addition to caring for a large house, garden, and family and sometimes a dog or two, running a small local nontraditional religious center, and sometimes even doing volunteer telephone counseling at the local mental health places; not to mention reading three or four books a week, and even taking the occasional course at the local community college in something which interests me, from hypnotism to music theory and harmony. There seems to be a level of about three thousand words a day beyond which I cannot increase my fiction output—that tops off at about fifteen to twenty pages a day. On a strictly temporary basis I can sometimes raise this amount—once for four days on end I wrote thirty-plus pages a day—but that was followed by a week or more of inactivity; the sponge had been squeezed dry and had to be refilled. I am no Erle Stanley Gardner or Barbara Cartland, to dictate a whole book over a weekend. The time I spent on fandom would have had to be filled with *something*, and it's hard to argue that I should have spent it knitting afghans or watching television. I did once write a novel in eleven days—but the less said about the quality of that particular book, the better!

So for myself, I can justify involvement in fandom. On the other hand, the person who holds a full-time job and is trying to write in his/her spare time, probably cannot justify this kind of involvement of time and energy unless he/she is deliberately holding back from taking the deepwater plunge into serious trails—writing and offering work for sale. I remember once telling Jacqueline Lichtenberg that it was time to stop wasting productive work hours (she had then two little children) on *Star*

Trek fiction and start using her time for serious professional work. Writers have all kinds of excuses for not writing, and getting committed to a heavy schedule of fannish activity is one of the best. I ought to know.

What are the other benefits of fandom to the actual or potential writer? The first, of course, is feedback. The fanzines are a good place to get your first work published, and to get into the habit of sitting there at the typewriter, of actually applying the seat of the pants to the seat of the chair and turning out words. For a beginner it is good to know that the editor needs your work so badly that he/she is not going to be critical. After a while you get to where turning out words is, quite literally, no sweat; you can sit down and just *do* it. When you agonize over every word because it might mean money or a chance at the big time, you may be too timid to write because if you wrote you'd have to submit it and if you submit it, it might get rejected. Writing for fanzines, less is at stake; even if you get rejected, you can say "Who the hell is *that* editor to reject *me*? Just a fan like me!" and the rejection isn't so serious. And when you have had a couple of hundred fanzine articles, letters, reviews, and stories in print, you begin to realize what writing is all about, and it's easier to expose yourself to the hard realities of the marketplace.

Another merit of the fanzines, especially the slick semipro ones that discriminate, is that they print very good and very select work, and pay at least a little. Someone used to say about vaudeville that it had the benefit of having, not only the Big Time, but an enormous number of what they then called "small time" for beginners; a place for neophytes and people just starting out in their chosen profession to be lousy in.

All writers write bad stories before they write good ones. (There are a few exceptions, but not many.) Or they write stories which are good in their own way, or acceptable to a narrower segment of the public, than the big commercial magazines must demand. Getting stories printed in a small-press magazine, even for a token honorarium of a quarter or half cent a word, gives the beginner confidence. The mechanism is the same as for the beginning voice student, studying in isolation, who grows depressed because he compares himself with Luciano Pavarotti. He needs to go on the recital stage to compare himself, not with a superstar, but with other young voice students who are not ready to audition even for the South Chicago Neighborhood Opera. So a young writer needs to compare himself, not with Ursula Le Guin or Harlan Ellison, but with Joe Fann. Such magazines as *Dragonfields*, *Shayol* and *Owlflight* serve a very real purpose. They have brought us, for instance, such writers as Charles Saunders and C. A. Cador.

Many writers nowadays make their way directly into the paperbacks, and go on from there. Ursula Le Guin, for instance, sold her first story directly as an Ace Double, and Michael Coney was discovered in Don Wollheim's slush pile, going on to write many good and valuable books. But for those who are not so lucky nor quite so talented, like myself, the apprenticeship of the fanzines was invaluable.

There are many other ways in which fandom can be helpful, other than providing first exposure for young talents. It is true that many professional editors read these "little magazines"—every now and then, a story turns up from one of them in the "Year's Best" anthologies. But even without that chance, fan writing and fan publishing provide friendship and understanding, the company of your peers, the reassurance of knowing others who share your aspirations and are on your wavelength—and that's only part of it.

Professional fiction, by its very nature, must appeal to a very broad base of interest; and this is more and more true as more publishers are swallowed up into conglomerates and distributed through mass-market places such as Waldenbooks and B. Dalton. I feel that by being accessible to my fans, I have given them a place to talk about some of the especially sensitive subjects on which I can only touch in my books. It is easier, and safer, for these young people to talk about women's rights, homosexuality, unusual approaches to religion, gender roles in society, and extrasensory perception on Darkover rather than in the worlds of suburbia or middle America where they themselves live. Many, perhaps most, of my fans live as misfits among their churchgoing, Barbara-Cartland-reading, soap-opera-watching peers, and find little support for any attempt at looking for a window on a larger and less constricted world of thought. I know how they feel. I too grew up in that kind of world and was emotionally battered when I tried to find something bigger and less constricted; and I found a world where I could find people who had thought about these things and were not afraid to talk about them. And the world I found was fandom.

I must confess myself quite partial in this assessment of fandom. I owe so much to fandom, from friendship to first exposure, from my first taste of professional confidence to a strong voice of support whenever I falter in my dedication to my chosen profession, that it would be worse than ungrateful to turn away from it. Some people seem to feel that at a certain age or professional level, a writer should turn his or her back on fandom, concentrating on professional activities only. Maybe they are right. I have never been very good, though, at doing what I "should" do. My latest fannish endeavor, editing the Darkover fiction magazine *Starstone*, sharpened my knowledge of how to write short fiction—by seeing others make all my mistakes, I was encouraged to avoid them, and for the first time in my life I can now write short stories and send them out *knowing* they will be sold. Until about five years ago, my short stories sold by accident, and I never knew why one story would sell and the other would pile up a dozen rejection slips. This endeavour led to the increase in my short-story sales, and also led to the editing of the two Darkover anthologies—which in turn seems to have led to the editing of a completely professional anthology which I have just turned in to DAW Books called *Sword and Sorceress*.

So even at this late date I am still learning from fandom, and will probably continue to do so. Give it up? Why? Would Judy Garland have given up "Over the Rainbow," even though she had "outgrown" it? It was a part of her image, a part of her professional life. As fandom is mine. And I think other writers are finding it so and will continue to find it valuable to their personal and professional lives for the foreseeable future.

I have stopped, therefore, apologizing for my continued involvement in fandom. I hope the day will come when other writers will be willing to give fandom its due, when there will be less snobbishness about fandom in this world we have all chosen to live in.

Granted, many fans are juvenile. But young people grow up. And it's true, fans can be a nuisance, and they can make heavy demands upon their idols. I once heard a writer, whom I will not name, bitching at a young fan for bringing a stack of books to an autographing party; the writer insisted that he would sign *one* hardcover, bought that day and not brought in from outside, and no more. A fan of mine, within earshot of that outburst, fearfully produced a grocery bag containing seven or eight books, and timidly asked if I really minded.

My answer was, "Hell, no. It's people like you who keep me in business."

Now that may not be *entirely* true. My books sell, in mass market, about a hundred times the number of copies which "Darkover fandom" alone could account for; for every book sold to a fan, a hundred and maybe a thousand go to people who have never heard of fandom, and this of course gives the writers I mentioned above the perfect excuse to ignore that fan and count on the 99 or 999 who buy their books anyhow. I could probably do the same without really hurting my sales figures all that much; for all I know, 95 percent or more of my royalties come from books bought by little old ladies to read on buses or while waiting in dentist's offices, and thrown away afterward. Although, of course, I get accused of exploiting my fans for sales. Not very long ago, a very bad review of my best-selling novel, *The Mists of Avalon*, implied—no, it came right out and said—that it had gotten on the best-seller lists only because I had circulated publicity so widely to the Friends of Darkover, and every Darkover fan had obviously bought copies. Now this, of course, is absolutely absurd. Even at its largest, Darkover fandom, taking in not only my own mailing list but everybody who has ever bought a copy of any Darkover fanzine, would encompass about fifteen hundred copies. That wouldn't have accounted for a quarter of the first printing; far less the seventy-five thousand copies or more which have sold. Nor would such papers as *The New York Times* been very likely to give favorable reviews because of the influence of Darkcover fandom—not a single Darkover novel has ever been mentioned in the *Times*.

But even so, I don't dismiss the articulate 1 percent who comprise fandom. How can I? The fan who cherishes a handful of battered, read-to-death paperbacks in long-out-of-print editions, who brings me at a convention a veritable suitcase full of everything I have ever written including a couple of my old Gothics, *that* fan is the hard core of the word-of-mouth which spreads my popularity. Because I know that fan is not only going to buy my book, but is going to buy copies for her sisters and her cousins and her aunts—and when someone asks her to recommend a book she is going to recommend one of mine. Should I, or could I, in common decency, be rude or ungracious to this person who has the good taste to appreciate what I am doing, and to tell me so? Some writers feel so sure of themselves that they kick their fans in the teeth. I've seen them doing to it, and listened to it, and it makes me cringe.

I'm not one of them. I am grateful to fandom because they listened to me and read me in fanzines and now they are reading me in a larger audience, I also know that any one of these young people could be, in ten or twenty years, standing where I am today; I see my own young self in them, wanting to know what made a Henry Kuttner or a Leigh Brackett or a Bob Mills tick. I am still very much one of them, and I don't feel at all degraded by remaining one of them.

One of the great dangers of being a writer is to grow old and out of touch with one's public. Recently I read part—a *small* part—of a novel by Robert Heinlein. His heroine "Friday" was not very different from his 1940s heroine, Podkayne of Mars. In forty years, more or less, Heinlein had learned little about the psychology of women. His more recent heroines talk more about sex, but they still talk in the language of the men's magazines of the forties; his women are not women but male delusions about women. The immensely popular best-selling author of the 1910–1918 world, Robert W. Chambers, vanished almost overnight from best-seller lists and went into almost total obscurity. Reading his contemporary mainstream novels of the twenties, it is easy to see why: he was still writing about the world of the twenties in the language of pre-war; he was an exact contemporary of D. H. Lawrence, yet his later novels were the same romantic fluff on which he had made his reputation. In the 1960s, it seemed that every other book on the newsstands was a "Gothic" novel. The writers who made their reputation on these formula stories are no longer writing them; readers want heroines, now, with enough sense to come in out of that gathering storm on the covers. I haven't seen an air-war pulp in thirty years. John D. MacDonald is now writing as well as ever about Travis McGee, but he doesn't write pulp thrillers any more, or he'd be starving instead of prosperous.

It is the phenomenon of fandom that keeps me in touch with this hard lesson for the writer. The writer who succumbs to the temptation to go for the sure thing, to write the same book over and over, without growth, experiment and failure—that writer will meet the fate of Chambers, and all the lost ladies who used to write Gothics; or he will, like Heinlein, be an object of scorn. Sure, Heinlein still sells, and people read his books, but I hear what the discriminating readers *say* about them. I don't want to wind up selling millions of books to people whose parents remembered that I was a great writer. His popularity is so great, his name so enormous, that he could sell a model spaceship kit cover with his name on it. But he is still writing for the fans and the audiences of the forties, and sooner or later it will catch up with him.

But if fans present the danger of keeping their idols frozen or locked into a single pattern, they also present a challenge and an opportunity. Fandom gives me the opportunity to hear the opinions of women younger than my own daughters; if I keep in touch with their needs and wants and tastes, I will not slip into the past, writing complacently of what I have always written, but will respond to what they are saying to me and of me. Some people think that in "Darkover fandom" I am simply surrounding myself with "adoring fans" and getting soothing strokes and endless egoboo (a fannish term for pridefully soliciting compliments, coming from the words "ego" and "boost"). That's far from true; my fans are my most challenging and demanding audience and never hesitate to let me know where I fall short of pleasing them. Some of them have attempted to prove, and actually proved, that they can write as well as I do myself in my own field. And certainly they give me plenty of blunt and challenging criticism.

In this sense I know that I can learn something, even from the most malicious and impertinent reviews. It is too easy to say that the writer of a bad review did not understand what I was trying to do. On a certain level, of course, a writer must disregard everything but his or her own highest standards; one cannot please everyone and a writer must eventually please oneself. Yet one must also listen to the displeasure as well as the flattery, or one is in the postion of the clergyman preaching only to the converted. If I have failed to reach a certain audience, why? Where and how have I failed to keep in touch with the needs of the audience?

The writer who listens can learn, like any performer, as much from the boos and whistles as from the thunder of applause. These are the straws in the wind that warn of changes in the needs of the readership, that demand a writer grow with changing times and changes in the readership, that help the perceptive writer to learn and grow. The writer, like any artist, who loses touch with the audience is already dead.

I want to live a long time.

Since earning his Ph. D. in American culture, Marshall B. Tymn has become an internationally recognized researcher in the science-fiction and fantasy fields. He has published twelve books and over thirty short pieces. He is an organizer of the Science Fiction Research Association, governor of the International Conference on the Fantastic in the Arts, and director of the National Workshop on Teaching Science Fiction.

Marshall Tymn wrote the next essay only because he had the good fortune to be visiting Lloyd Biggle. Lloyd and I were on the phone, discussing not only Lloyd's essay but my search for someone "with credentials" who could write a specific piece on science fiction in the schools. My second problem was that I needed the essay right away.

Lloyd replied, "Don't worry. Marshall Tymn will be walking through my front door within the hour. He teaches teachers about science fiction and he can write your essay."

So here it is. . . .

7
SCIENCE FICTION IN THE CLASSROOM
MARSHALL B. TYMN

Once exiled to comic strips, pulp magazines, and late-night movies, science fiction is fast becoming not only "respectable" but the most popular of the specialized literary genres in the United States today. Its enthusiasts range from omnivorous devourers of paperbacks to serious scholars who probe, analyze, and discuss the characteristics and significance of works old and new.

The reason for this explosion of interest is not just fascination with exotic settings and futuristic worlds. Science fiction is being recognized—and this is especially true in the schools—as a literature that prepares us to accept change, to view change as both natural and inevitable. And since change is fast becoming one of the few constants in our society, the attractiveness of this genre is both understandable and encouraging. Add the popular appeal that science fiction has as pure entertainment, and it becomes clear why this literature is attracting vast numbers of readers of all ages and from all stations of life.

The May 1984 issue of *Science Fiction Chronicle* reports that, according to annual sales figures in the March 16 *Publishers Weekly*, science fiction and fantasy were among the top hardcover and paperback bestsellers during 1983. Of the top twenty hardcover sellers of 1983, six were science fiction or fantasy.[1] *PW* also reported that nine mass-market science fiction/fantasy paperbacks had sales of one million or more copies during 1983.[2] In all, over 1,085 volumes of science fiction and fantasy were published in 1983, a banner year according to *Locus* magazine (February 1984). Of these, 581 were original publications, accounting for about 15 per cent of all the fiction published in the United States. The publishing industry is frantic with activity, with well over a hundred book publishers supporting the work of more writers than the field has ever known, many of whom now routinely receive five-figure advances (with a few six-figures lurking in the background).[3]

In addition, a number of magazines publish the work of established writers and provide a marketplace for promising new talent. The established leaders in the field are *Analog, Isaac Asimov's Science Fiction Magazine, The Magazine of Fantasy & Science Fiction, The Twilight Zone*, and *Omni*.

The current wide range of science-fiction fan activities is another indicator of just how popular this literature has become in recent years. Fandom exerts a strong influence on the science-fiction field through its awards, its conventions, and the development of new writers and editors. Scores of conventions on local, regional, and national levels are held each year in the United States, where fans and professionals gather to share their mutual admiration for science fiction. (The 1983 World Science Fiction Convention in Baltimore attracted nearly seven thousand persons.) No other form of literature offers such numerous opportunities for readers to meet and socialize with their favorite authors while at the same time sharing opinions and ideas via panel discussions and open forums.

Motion pictures, too, have helped enlarge the science fiction community by attracting new readers to the fold, while other media, including radio, television, and the theater, have produced science fiction for mass audiences.

The science-fiction boom, now fully upon us, has been growing since the early 1970s, when science-fiction fandom came of age and when the publishing industry began to issue titles in record numbers. The scope of activity in the science-fiction field is now so immense that *Locus*, the award-winning "newspaper of the science-fiction field," has expanded its monthly coverage to over fifty pages. For those who want regular coverage of the activities and publications in both science fiction and fantasy, *Locus* is indeed indispensable.[4] (Another useful and informative monthly review of current events in the science fiction field is *Science Fiction Chronicle*, mentioned above.)

Alongside the growth of science fiction as a popular literature has been its gradual emergence and acceptance as an academic discipline. In 1970, the Science Fiction Research Association was established to encourage and assist scholarship in the field.[5] At about the same time, courses in science fiction began to proliferate, and there was a noticeable increase in the publication of works of criticism and reference to meet the demands of the scholar and teacher. Special sections on science fiction are now regular features on the programs of academic organizations such as the Modern Language Association, the National Council of Teachers of English, and the Popular Culture Association. Scholarly journals such as *Extrapolation* (US), *Science-Fiction Studies* (Canada), *Foundation* (UK) and *Science Fiction* (Australia) serve the science-fiction community, along with excellent magazines of review and general commentary like *Fantasy Review*.[6]

The genre was given further impetus in 1980 when the International Conference on the Fantastic in the Arts was established by Dr. Robert A. Collins and a staff at Florida Atlantic University. Now the largest conference of its kind in the field, its annual meetings, controlled by the International Association for the Fantastic in the Arts, have become the major focal point for the dissemination of scholarship in science fiction, fantasy and horror literature among a wide range of specialized and traditional disciplines.[7]

This growing acceptance of science fiction at all levels has resulted in a demand for new science-fiction courses in secondary schools, junior colleges, and universities. Two national workshops have been organized to familiarize educators with the responsibilities of teaching science fiction. Begun in 1975 at Eastern Michigan University under my direction, the annual Workshop on Teaching Science Fiction & Fantasy is now the only ongoing weekend teacher-training facility in the United States. The workshop is designed to disseminate the latest information, methods and materials, and to provide a forum for the exchange of ideas on teaching science fiction. Beginning in 1981, the workshop became a permanent part of the program of the International Conference on the Fantastic in the Arts.[8]

Organized in 1977 at the University of Kansas by Dr. James Gunn, the Intensive English Institute on the Teaching of Science Fiction offers teachers the opportunity to familiarize themselves with the history and significance of the science-fiction genre as well as more advanced areas of reading, interpretation, and teaching. The course work provides a complete survey of science fiction, an understanding of what science fiction is and how it works, how it functions as literature, and how it can be taught. This program offers graduate credit.[9]

As a workshop director I receive many inquiries from science-fiction teachers, not only about teaching methods, but about resource materials and where they can be found. I can sympathize fully with the problems encountered by the new teacher, as I have taught at least two sections of science fiction per academic year (sometimes as many as five) since 1974, when I organized the course and became its sole proprietor at Eastern Michigan University. I would like to devote the rest of this essay to answering the most-often-asked questions by new science-fiction teachers. Taken as a whole they represent a broad range of concerns that isolate some of the problems facing the teacher in today's science-fiction classroom. My responses to these queries comprise the basic structure of my workshop and are discussed in more detail in my *Teacher's Guide to Fantastic Literature*.[10]

1: Why teach science fiction?

A useful starting point in any workshop, this question may seem obvious to an experienced teacher, but difficult to express for one approaching the study of science fiction for the first time. One of the obvious responses to this question is that science fiction is exciting and entertaining. This no one would deny. Those stories of heroism and survival on hostile alien worlds or in the deeps of space that characterized the literature in its formative years are still with us today in all their infinite variety. Science fiction is fun to read. But is this enough? For some readers, and perhaps for some students, it is. Many teachers I encounter, though, demand more of the works they offer in the classroom. Science-fiction writer and educator Jack Williamson says that "the most successful teachers are motivated by a sense that science fiction has a special relevance to life in our transitional times." Because science fiction portrays a multitude of alternate futures, it can provide students not only with a means for evaluating the forces affecting the shape the future may take, but also with extrapolations depicting various directions in which advances in science and technology may lead us. These alternate futures can also provide the perspective needed to appreciate the possibilities open to society and the human race—a vision not always easy to achieve in our rapidly changing environment.

Although to some extent the movies and TV have misled people into believing that science fiction's primary concern is with bug-eyed monsters, mechanical mutants, and epic battles in space, contemporary science fiction has evolved into a literature of serious social commentary—even while preserving its origins of romantic escapism and intriguing gadgetry. Its writers are examining the human consequences of technology, overpopulation, governmental abuses of power, racial conflict, and a host of other social themes. Beyond its concern with outer space and alien environments, science fiction is looking more closely at life on our home planet.

It is precisely this attitude that makes the literature so popular. In their concern for how their lives in the future will be affected by changes occurring in society today, students have turned to science fiction not just because it is extremely exciting, but because it can help them to deal with what is happening today and will be happening tomorrow. Therein lies the challenge for today's science-fiction teacher.

2: What teaching aids are currently available?

One of the problems facing the new teacher is the difficulty in obtaining current information on the practical applications of organizing science-fiction courses. I spend a large amount of time in my workshops helping teachers plan their syllabi. This is not always the easiest of tasks, as science-fiction courses vary as widely as the departments in which they are taught, which range from the sciences through humanities and the social sciences. A number of teacher resource materials were published in the early 1970s, when the first big wave of new science-fiction courses was felt in academic circles. In my chapter, "Teaching Aids," in Neil Barron's *Anatomy of Wonder: A Critical Guide to Science Fiction* (Bowker, 1981), I discuss these resource materials, all of which were published between 1972 and 1977. Although none of these books and pamphlets was very comprehensive, they were prepared for the most part by people with some knowledge of the field and did provide background information combined with a few practical teaching suggestions. As useful starting points these publications served a real need. Unfortunately, nearly everything that was published during this period is out of print today, and there have been no guides published since to replace them, unless one counts James Gunn's excellent teacher's manual which accompanies his anthology series, *The Road to Science Fiction* or my own *A Teacher's Guide to Fantastic Literature* (now privately printed), discussed in note 10 at the end of this essay.

To the best of my knowledge, these guides are still available: L. David Allen's *Science Fiction: An Introduction* (Cliff Notes, 1973), Kenneth Donelson's *Science Fiction in the English Class* (NCTE, 1972), and Sylvia Spann and Mary Beth Culp's *Thematic Units in Teaching English and the Humanities* ("The Future Arrives before the Present Has Left," NCTE, 1975).

Beginning in the early 1970s, a number of audiovisual materials were produced, and unlike the teaching guides, many of these films, filmstrips, slide/sound sets, records and audiotapes are still available. Audiovisual aids can help motivate not only the reluctant student but the inexperienced teacher. These programs are general guides to the science-fiction genre, and as such serve mainly to stimulate further, more intense discussions of historical movements, themes, works, and the like. They cannot substitute for informed and enthusiastic teaching, but as supplements, aids, and motivation-reinforcing tools, these materials can provide meaningful and stimulating classroom experiences to suit a variety of student-teacher needs and backgrounds. Of the eleven programs I discuss in detail in *Anatomy of Wonder*, two are excellent all-purpose surveys of the genre, designed especially for introductory courses: *Science Fiction and Fantasy* (two color filmstrips, two cassettes or records, Educational Audio Visual, 1976) and *Science Fiction: Jules Verne to Ray Bradbury* (240 slides, three cassettes or records, Center for Humanities, 1974). For a complete listing of audiovisual materials suitable for use in the science-fiction classroom, see my "Guide to AV Resources in Science Fiction and Fantasy" in the November 1979 issue of *Media & Methods*. This bibliography contains capsule summaries of all programs ever produced, an index to titles and authors, and addresses of all publishers and producers.

Thanks to the efforts of Jack Williamson, there now exists a general orientation tool for science-fiction teachers. *Teaching Science Fiction: Education for Tomorrow* (Owlswick Press, 1980) is a collection of essays that provides background information for the teacher of science fiction from elementary through college level. Twenty-five essays include material on the origins and evolution of science fiction, its significance and literary values, used in various subject disciplines, and resources available to the teacher. This book is packed with informed commentary and should be read by every science-fiction teacher no matter how long he or she has been teaching.

3: What are the best ways to organize a science fiction course?

In the absence of published practical guidelines, those teachers who have not had the opportunity to attend a workshop must sometimes resort to "hit-or-miss" methods of organizing their courses. This can result in a hasty, ill-conceived syllabus which may turn off the brighter students. Because of the diverse subject matter of science fiction, there is no universally accepted methodology for organizing stories and novels into ideal teaching units. But there are *starting points* which the teacher who is familiar with the literature can adept to his or her needs. I would like to introduce four basic approaches to teaching science fiction; none is mutually exclusive, but each is distinct and can be modified to suit particular curriculum requirements and student needs.

A. HISTORICAL

This method traces the historical development of science fiction from a relevant starting point (e.g., Mary Shelley's *Frankenstein*, 1818) to present writings in the field, but does not concentrate heavily on contemporary works. As a variation, any period in science-fiction history could be emphasized, such as the first so-called "Golden Age" (1938–1950) or the New Wave movement of the 1960s. In this approach to course structure, *a coherent sense of history* should underlie the teacher's selection of materials. A historical anthology should be used, supplemented with novels and background discussions and/or films on the development of the genre. The ideal anthology for this approach is James Gunn's *The Road to Science Fiction*, as it is packed with useful historical commentary which ideally complements the story selections. As a practical exercise, I ask my students to outline this material throughout the duration of the course; the outline is refined as the material is discussed, and model works suggested by Gunn and myself are plugged into the outline. The student ends up with an overview of the history of the genre and a chronology of important science-fiction works. A syllabus for such a course could be extracted from the following model, which contains more titles than could possibly be offered in a one-semester class.[11]

HISTORICAL

James Gunn, *THE ROAD TO SCIENCE FICTION* (4 vols.)
Norman Spinrad, *MODERN SCIENCE FICTION*
Robert Silverberg, *THE MIRROR OF INFINITY*
Eric S. Rabkin, *SCIENCE FICTION: A HISTORICAL ANTHOLOGY*

BACKGROUNDS: BEFORE 1926

Mary Shelley, *FRANKENSTEIN*
Jules Verne, *FROM THE EARTH TO THE MOON*
H. G. Wells, *THE WAR OF THE WORLDS*
Edgar Rice Burroughs, *A PRINCESS OF MARS*

THE AGE OF WONDER: 1926–1937

Edward E. Smith, *THE SKYLARK OF SPACE*
Edwin Balmer/Philip Wylie, *WHEN WORLDS COLLIDE*

THE GOLDEN AGE: 1938–1949

Isaac Asimov, *THE FOUNDATION TRILOGY*
A. E. van Vogt, *THE WORLD OF NULL-A*
Clifford D. Simak, *CITY*

THE AGE OF ACCEPTANCE: 1950–1961

Frederik Pohl/C. M. Kornbluth, *THE SPACE MERCHANTS*
Arthur C. Clarke, *CHILDHOOD'S END*
Hal Clement, *MISSION OF GRAVITY*
Ray Bradbury, *FAHRENHEIT 451*
Edgar Pangborn, *A MIRROR FOR OBSERVERS*
Robert A. Heinlein, *STARSHIP TROOPERS*
Harry Harrison, *DEATHWORLD TRILOGY*
Brian W. Aldiss, *STARSHIP*

THE AGE OF REBELLION: 1962–1973

John Brunner, *STAND ON ZANZIBAR*
Thomas M. Disch, *CAMP CONCENTRATION*

Frank Herbert, *DUNE*
Ursula K. Le Guin, *THE LEFT HAND OF DARKNESS*
Robert Silverberg, *DYING INSIDE*

B. MAJOR WORKS

A Major Works approach surveys key works in the development of science fiction from a selected starting point in its history. This method tends to overlap with the Historical approach, although one's choice of major works need not depend on historical criteria. Works selected as "major" should be based on *defensible* selection criteria, i.e., award winners, or works indicative of a particular type or style. Because of the relative difficulty in establishing "firm" reasons for works included in this syllabus, the teacher should have more than a passing acquaintance with the history of the literature; without this background one's choices of major works will be less objective and more open to charges of "favoritism." A useful anthology for this type of course would be one, like those listed in the sample syllabus below, that contains stories generally regarded as representative of the genre. The novels in this syllabus should be accepted by readers and critics as key works in the field.

MAJOR WORKS

Robert Silverberg, *SCIENCE FICTION HALL OF FAME*, Vol. I
Ben Bova, *THE SCIENCE FICTION HALL OF FAME*, Vols. IIA—IIB
Isaac Asimov, *THE HUGO AWARD WINNERS* (3 vols.)
SFWA, *NEBULA AWARD STORIES*
H. G. Wells, *THE TIME MACHINE*
George Stewart, *EARTH ABIDES*
Alfred Bester, *THE DEMOLISHED MAN*
Theodore Sturgeon, *MORE THAN HUMAN*
Walter M. Miller, Jr., *A CANTICLE FOR LEIBOWITZ*
Frank Herbert, *DUNE*
Robert A. Heinlein, *STRANGER IN A STRANGE LAND*
Brian W. Aldiss, *THE LONG AFTERNOON OF EARTH*
Clifford D. Simak, *WAY STATION*
Daniel Keyes, *FLOWERS FOR ALGERNON*
Larry Niven, *RINGWORLD*
Philip K. Dick, *THE MAN IN THE HIGH CASTLE*

Ursula K. Le Guin, *THE DISPOSSESSED*
Vonda N. McIntyre, *DREAMSNAKE*

C. THEMATIC

In the Thematic approach, reading assignments are selected on the basis of their classification into a certain subject area. Works chosen should be representative of their type, not exceptions to it. This method of organization reinforces the fact that science fiction is a subject-matter-oriented literature. Themes can be grouped around novels, a thematic anthology, or a comprehensive general anthology. Most thematic anthologies are too restrictive, as they tend to be organized around a single theme. I prefer a good general anthology, such as *Science Fiction Hall of Fame*, whose contents can be rearranged according to motif by the teacher (a fun exercise in isolating the major focus of the story). Sharing information on the development of each theme in science-fiction literature will provide students with the needed historical perspective on each motif and stimulate class discussion by examining other works in each thematic category. Background information on the major themes can be found in Peter Nicholls's *The Science Fiction Encyclopedia* (Doubleday, 1979).

THEMATIC

Robert Silverberg/Martin H. Greenberg, *THE ARBOR HOUSE TREASURY OF MODERN SCIENCE FICTION*
Robert Silverberg, *SCIENCE FICTION HALL OF FAME*, Vol. I

SPACE ADVENTURE

Larry Niven/Jerry Pournelle, *THE MOTE IN GOD'S EYE*
Poul Anderson, *TAU ZERO*

ALIEN CULTURES

C. J. Cherryh, *BROTHERS OF EARTH*
F. M. Busby, *CAGE A MAN*

POST-CATASTROPHE

Vonda N. McIntyre, *DREAMSNAKE*
Chelsea Quinn Yarbro, *FALSE DAWN*

TIME TRAVEL

Gordon R. Dickson, *TIME STORM*
Robert Silverberg, *UP THE LINE*

ALTERNATE WORLDS

Brian W. Aldiss, *THE MALACIA TAPESTRY*
Norman Spinrad, *THE IRON DREAM*

ARTIFICIAL LIFE

Philip K. Dick, *WE CAN BUILD YOU*
Jack Williamson, *THE HUMANOID TOUCH*

TECHNOLOGY

Arthur C. Clarke, *THE FOUNTAINS OF PARADISE*
John Varley, *THE OPHIUCHI HOTLINE*
Frederik Pohl, *MAN PLUS*

FUTURE WAR

Joe Haldeman, *THE FOREVER WAR*
Jerry Pournelle, *THE MERCENARY*

D. MAJOR AUTHORS (CONTEMPORARY)

A Major Authors syllabus can obviously begin anywhere from H. G. Wells onward. This is perhaps the most difficult of the four approaches because it overlaps with the others to some extent. But if one limits one's selections to contemporary writers, overlapping is not an important concern. I have found the Major Authors (Contemporary) a popular approach in my university classes, which are populated mainly by students who want to read the "good stuff" and who have a limited amount of time to spend on pleasure reading. Students these days seem to want to read stimulating, well-written works, according to the comments I receive in workshops; they are no longer satisfied with poorly written books with stale themes—they get enough triteness in the movies. This is not to say that a prudent selection of older works will not provide provocative reading. But contemporary works as a whole represent remarkable advances in literary quality and offer a more sophisticated range of relevant subject matter. Historical background can be supplied, if necessary, with a lecture or film.[12] Students expect some sort of background information in *any* science-fiction course, no matter how it is organized. It can be brief and serve as a starting point for a discussion of contemporary science fiction, or it can be a detailed and integral part of the course—but do offer them some material on our literary history. Information on fandom could also be introduced in this unit, since so many contemporary authors are involved in it. Anthologies for a Major Authors (Contemporary) course should be selected for their literary merit, such as the two standards listed in the model syllabus below.

MAJOR AUTHORS (CONTEMPORARY)

Terry Carr, *THE BEST SCIENCE FICTION OF THE YEAR*
Donald A. Wollheim, *THE . . . ANNUAL WORLD'S BEST SF*
Robert Silverberg, *A TIME OF CHANGES*
Kate Wilhelm, *WHERE LATE THE SWEET BIRDS SANG*
Frederik Pohl, *GATEWAY*
Gregory Benford, *TIMESCAPE*
Joan D. Vinge, *THE SNOW QUEEN*
Gene Wolfe, *THE SHADOW OF THE TORTURER*
C. J. Cherryh, *DOWNBELOW STATION*
John Varley, *MILLENIUM*

In each of these approaches to course structure, emphasis should be placed on the use of *quality* science fiction. All works selected, furthermore, should conform to a working definition of science fiction (which can be discussed in class) and even prove exemplary of the genre. This places great responsibility on the selection skills of the teacher.

In all cases, choose works that are *teachable*, i.e., they develop their subject in an interesting and plausible manner, demonstrate outstanding literary merit, possess enough thematic significance to stimulate class discussion, focus on at least one narrative element or device important to good literature, and above all, *entertain*.

4: Is there such a thing as a standard classroom text for introductory science-fiction courses?

Anyone familiar with fantastic literature knows that the field is glutted with anthologies; this is a result of the genre's emphasis on short fiction. Few of these anthologies, however, are designed with the classroom teacher in mind. The lists of "texts" is small and is growing smaller each year, as one after another goes out of print. Publishers seem unwilling to take a chance on a so-called class text, which they claim has a "restricted" market, yet scores of mass-market and trade anthologies appear each year and disappear after a few weeks on the bookstore shelves. Lloyd Biggle, Jr., a noted science-fiction writer who has maintained a deep interest in the impact of science fiction in education, remarks that "textbook publishers continue to maintain that there is no market for science fiction texts. There is an enormous market; but because the publishers are unwilling or unable to supply texts that appeal to the teachers, the market is being filled from the regular paperbacks racks."

Of the fourteen science-fiction anthologies I discuss in *Anatomy of Wonder*, only eight are still in print and are listed below.[13] Of these, I can only recommend *three* (marked with an asterisk) for use in science-fiction classes today:

*Dick Allen, *SCIENCE FICTION: THE FUTURE* (Harcourt Brace Jovanovich, rev. ed. 1983). General, futurology.

*James Gunn, *THE ROAD TO SCIENCE FICTION*, 4 vols. (NAL, 1977, 1979, 1982). Historical, broad range.

Bonnie L. Heintz, et al. *TOMORROW, AND TOMORROW, AND TOMORROW* (Holt, Rinehart and Winston, 1974). Thematic, narrow range.

Leo P. Kelley, *THEMES IN SCIENCE FICTION* (McGraw-Hill, 1972). Thematic, medium range.

Donald L. Lawler, *APPROACHES TO SCIENCE FICTION* (Houghton Mifflin, 1978). General.

Fred Obrecht, *SCIENCE FICTION AND FANTASY: 26 CLASSIC AND CONTEMPORARY STORIES* (Barron's Educational Series, 1977). General.

Eric S. Rabkin, *SCIENCE FICTION: A HISTORICAL ANTHOLOGY* (Oxford, 1983). Historical, wide range.

Thomas E. Sanders, *SPECULATIONS: AN INTRODUCTION TO LITERATURE THROUGH FANTASY AND SCIENCE FICTION* (Glencoe, 1973). General.

*Charles Wm. Sullivan III. *AS TOMORROW BECOMES TODAY* (Prentice-Hall, 1974). Thematic, broad range.

Patricia Warrick, et al. *SCIENCE FICTION: CONTEMPORARY MYTHOLOGY: THE SFWA-SFRA ANTHOLOGY* (Harper & Row, 1978). Thematic, broad range.

Because of this paucity of useful texts, many science-fiction teachers (including myself) have successfully employed mass-market anthologies in the classroom. (Most of the anthologies listed in my model syllabi above are mass-market titles.) There are a variety of anthology types, yet a wise choice by the teacher can result in an inexpensive, representative selection of modern science fiction. Stick to the nonspecialized titles, which are better suited for survey courses—and check to see if your title is available from the publisher *before* you order it.

5: What are the classic science-fiction works?

In a literature as relatively "new" as science fiction, I'm not sure the word "classic" can be applied. Some modern works have transcended their subject matter with universal themes that appeal to a wide and diverse audience. Titles like the following have survived the "test of time" and could be regarded as classics: Arthur C. Clarke, *Childhood's End*; Frank Herbert, *Dune*; Walter M. Miller, Jr., *A Canticle for Leibowitz*; Ursula K. Le Guin, *The Left Hand of Darkness*; Philip K. Dick, *The Man in the High Castle*; Ray Bradbury, *The Martian Chronicles*. The list goes on.

Other works have immense historical importance to the genre and could be regarded as classics in another sense. Examples are: H. G. Wells, *The War of the Worlds*; George Orwell, *1984*; Isaac Asimov, *The Foundation Trilogy*; Frederik Pohl and C. M. Kornbluth, *The Space Merchants*; Theodore Sturgeon, *More Than Human*; Clifford D. Simak, *City*; Robert A. Heinlein, *Stranger in a Strange Land*, plus many others.

What is or isn't a science-fiction classic is still largely a matter of personal judgment, and lists of such works vary widely. New teachers are sometimes apt to design a syllabus "packed" with the so-called classics of the genre, especially if they are works they once read or ones that seem to be associated with the genre in the popular mind. Such a syllabus might look something like this:

> Jules Verne, *20,000 LEAGUES UNDER THE SEA*
> H. G. Wells, *THE TIME MACHINE*
> Aldous Huxley, *BRAVE NEW WORLD*
> George Orwell, *1984*
> Ray Bradbury, *THE MARTIAN CHRONICLES*
> Isaac Asimov, *I, ROBOT*
> Michael Crichton, *THE ANDROMEDA STRAIN*

There are many problems associated with such a list, not the least of which is that as a whole it is not representative of the current state of the art. Don't fall into this trap yourself—and think of your students!

6: I have just been told I will be teaching science fiction next fall. What can I do during the summer to prepare for this assignment?

Read science fiction! Night and day! The best preparation a teacher can possibly hope to have is to know the literature. Well-read teachers have far fewer problems and don't run scared all semester. No amount of studying the available resources or reading in the history of science fiction will get the teacher past the classroom door if he or she hasn't read widely in the field. Lloyd Biggle has observed that "unfortunately, the explosion of courses may result in science fiction being taught by teachers who have little or no previous knowledge of the subject. High school mini-courses are often staff-planned, with the sections taught by volunteers—or by teachers who are volunteered for the job." At my own workshops, there are always a number of panicky attendees who know nothing about science fiction but have suddenly been handed the job of teaching it. Sadly, students will suffer (and the course may fail) because some teachers lack both interest and background in science fiction.

Where to begin reading? Start with the Hugo and Nebula Award winners and go on from there. An excellent starting point is *A History of the Hugo, Nebula and International Fantasy Awards*, compiled by Donald Franson and Howard DeVore. This informative booklet provides title listings of both the winners and nominees in all categories of these awards and can be used as a comprehensive core reading list and as an aid for course preparation.[14]

7: What kind of students will I meet in my science-fiction class?

Perhaps one-half of your students will be brand new to the field, with no previous familiarity with it apart from their exposure to movies and TV, but who are curious about science fiction for a number of reasons. One-fourth will be occasional readers who, perhaps like yourself, are familiar with a few of the most popular titles. The other one-fourth range from fairly regular readers to the hard-core buffs, who read science fiction constantly. Many of these devotees possess an encyclopedic knowledge of everything they have ever read, and if the teacher is not intimidated by these buffs, they can be invaluable as discussion leaders and resource persons. Science-fiction readers come from many different backgrounds and life-styles. Don't begin your class with any preconceived ideas of what science fiction readers are like—you'll be wrong every time.

8: How will be colleagues react to me now that I am a science-fiction teacher?

Probably very strangely. Science fiction teachers have told me that they have been ridiculed, even abused, by their colleagues, who are all too eager to challenge the validity of the new science-fiction course. One reason for such an attitude is sheer jealousy over the immense popularity of science fiction with the students. The other, as Lloyd Biggle puts it, "is an arrogant stupidity masquerading as ignorance." Although this problem is more apparent on the college and university levels, it is noticeable in the public schools, too. Science fiction teachers must be prepared to confront the widespread notion that science fiction is not literature, and should therefore not be taught in the schools.

Thanks to the pervasive influence of organizations such as the Science Fiction Research Association and the International Association for the Fantastic in the Arts, science fiction as a literary genre has had an impact on traditional scholarship in recent years, an impact which, at scholarly meetings and in the learned journals, has helped to dispel those nasty rumors that science fiction is inferior to all other forms of literature. The situation for science fiction has improved remarkably during the past ten years, and will continue to improve as more and more teachers enter the field to spread "the gospel from outer space."

NOTES

[1] Leading the list as the best hardcover seller of 1983 was *Return of the Jedi Storybook*, by Joan D. Vinge. #3 was Stephen King's *Pet Sematary*, #5 was King's *Christine*, #8 was *White Gold Wielder* by Stephen R. Donaldson, #12, *The Robots of Dawn* by Isaac Asimov, and #15, *Moreta: Dragonlady of Pern* by Anne McCaffrey.

[2] The mass-market paperback best-sellers are *Cujo, Christine* and *Different Seasons* by Stephen King; *Space* by James Michener; *The Valley of Horses* by Jean Auel; *Life, The Universe and Everything* by Douglas Adams; *Foundation's Edge* by Isaac Asimov; *God Emperor of Dune* by Frank Herbert; and *The Keep* by F. Paul Wilson.

[3] Six-figure advances, although still relatively uncommon, are occurring more often. It is a sign that the publishing industry is more willing than ever to spend large sums of money to promote science fiction and fantasy.

[4] For subscription information, write Locus Publications, Box 13305, Oakland, CA 94661. The address of *Science Fiction Chronicle* is Box 4175, New York, NY 10163-4175.

[5] Those wishing to join SFRA may do so by writing the treasurer, Donald M. Hassler, 1226 Woodhill Dr., Kent, OH 44240.

[6] Subscriptions to *Extrapolation, Science-Fiction Studies* and *Fantasy Review* are included in the SFRA membership package.

[7] Information on IAFA, its annual meetings and publications, may be obtained by writing its president, Roger C. Schlobin, 802 N. Calumet, Chesterton, IN 46304.

[8] The next national workshop will be offered in conjunction with the March 1985 annual meeting of the International Conference on the Fantastic in the Arts. Advance enrollments are accepted and may be confirmed by writing Marshall B. Tymn, 721 Cornell, Ypsilani, MI 48197 for information.

[9] If you are interested in attending the Institute, write James Gunn for a brochure at the English Department, The University of Kansas, Lawrence, KS 66045.

[10] This is the only comprehensive guide to teaching science fiction currently available. Published by Florida Atlantic University for use in my annual workshops, it is now being considered by a commercial publisher and could be available sometime in 1985. If you would like to be included on a mailing list to receive this guide when it becomes available, send me your name and address.

[11] The categories used in this model historical syllabus are from Lester del Rey's *The World of Science Fiction* (Garland, 1980). With sufficient background reading in the history of science fiction, the teacher can construct his/her own labels.

[12] Audiovisual aids for science fiction teachers are discussed in my *Anatomy of Wonder* chapter, "Teaching Aids."

[13] See also this chapter for detailed comments on these and other texts not listed here.

[14] To order this valuable booklet, send five dollars to Howard DeVore, 4705 Weddel, Dearborn, MI 48125.

Two events got me where I am today.

The first occurred over twenty-five years ago, when my mother gave me her library card. It enabled me to read through certain previously forbidden sections of the local library before I reached puberty: science fiction, occult, psychology, sociology, and religion.

The second was losing my job on a weekly newspaper when one publisher threw the other down a flight of stairs and the employees came back after lunch to find all the doors padlocked and guarded by someone carrying an axe handle.

Shortly after this bizarre scenario, I was offered a position as a secretary for the travel section of *The New York Times*. Though this was fifteen years ago, I was somewhat of a feminist even then, and the application "secretary" did not sit well with me. I was used to bylines, so I turned down the *Times* and went into books. Sometimes I think I may have made a mistake.

Back then, book publishing was touted as being both creative and romantic. Think of all those famous literary figures I would soon be taking to lunch . . . and if I got to work on my favorite reading matter, science fiction, well—imagine, getting paid to have fun!

Unfortunately there were some glitches to this idyllic existence. When I found out what really went on behind the scenes and in corporate meeting rooms, that's when I learned what fantasy really was. . . .

8

WHAT DOES A WOMAN KNOW ABOUT SCIENCE FICTION, ANYWAY?

SHARON JARVIS

Little girls do not grow up thinking, "I'm going to be the next Maxwell Perkins." Unless, of course, they know who Maxwell Perkins is. (For the benefit of the uninformed, he was one of the twentieth century's most acclaimed book editors.) And little girls do not find themselves editing science fiction unless it is through a strange turn of events. And, perhaps, a strange turn of mind as well. . . .

It began in 1969, when I was hired by Ace Books as a copyeditor. In case you don't know it, a copyeditor is responsible for all the grammar, spelling, punctuation, and continuity in some poor author's manuscript. I was hired because I was a college grad with some experience (see: newspaper, demise of).

Ace quickly handed me a blue pencil, a *Manual of Style*, and a science-fiction manuscript.

My superior was Donald A. Wollheim, editor-in-chief and extraordinary person. Don was already a luminary in the science-fiction field, a member of First Fandom, an editor and writer, and had persuaded Ace to publish large numbers of books in the genre. In fact, Ace was one of the leading publishers of science fiction. Guiding them was Don, the dedicated fan, who also knew how to make money.

Don Wollheim taught me a lot about science fiction and about science-fiction publishing, but the most important thing he ever taught me was about book covers. As editor-in-chief, Don had complete control over cover art. He would always instruct the art director to make sure that every science-fiction book showed at least one alien or one spaceship—preferably both.

I took these words to heart: when I later edited science fiction and fantasy at Playboy Books, I made sure that every science fiction cover had a strange creature or rockets, and if none were in the story, it got added. For example, the winged cat woman on the cover of *In the Shadow of Omizantrim* (Book Five of *The War of Powers* series by Vardeman and Milan) never existed in the original outline. I took Bob Vardeman to lunch in a very fancy restaurant and explained the Wollheim Rule over dessert. We concocted a bizarre creature for the express purpose of illustrating it on the cover; it worked and the book sold very well.

So aside from the Westerns and nurse novels which I also copyedited, I had a wonderful time working on science fiction at Ace Books. The only drawback was that Ace had no room for me. For several weeks I had to share an office with one of their editors, Terry Carr.

Terry Carr is one of the field's most famous editors and anthologists, so I hid in the corner and tried not to disturb him. Most of the time, though, it was Terry who had me in quiet hysterics, as I heroically tried not to laugh out loud. Since Terry spent considerable time on the phone with the acerbic and volatile Harlan Ellison, "discussing" the Science Fiction Writers of America and their upcoming Nebula Awards, I usually had a blue pencil in my right hand while my left hand was over my mouth.

Many well-known writers in the field often came up to see Don and Terry. Barry Malzberg was a regular visitor and advisor; Ron Goulart came up with a new book every three months; Isaac Asimov and Marion Zimmer Bradley phoned often; Lin Carter came to visit. Consequently, many people who formerly were just names on book covers became real to me.

But while I was in science-fiction heaven, I eventually woke up to some publishing facts of life. All the so-called "male" books were edited by men. These included science fiction, Westerns, mysteries, thrillers, and action-adventure books. Evelyn Grippo, Ace's other acquisitions editor, was responsible for all kinds of women's fiction, including romances, historicals, gothics, and the stomach-turning nurse novels.

After I left Ace, and, still later, when Don Wollheim left to start his own publishing company, Ace cast about for a new science fiction editor. Naturally, they searched for an available *male* editor since, as we all know, science fiction is read only by fourteen-year-old boys. They found their new editor in the mailroom.

That's another old publishing maxim: men can work their way up from the mailroom but women begin as secretaries. I knew exactly one woman who made it from secretary to vice president, but it had taken twenty-five years. I couldn't wait that long.

The only way to earn a living wage in publishing was to quit and go elsewhere, so I left and went to Popular Library. Its employees affectionately referred to the company as Popular Paranoia. (It was so weird there that I went back to Don Wollheim and apologized for anything I had ever said about Ace.) At Popular Library I learned a few more publishing facts. Publishers have lots of female help because they can pay them less money, but the people in power are always men. The acquisitions editor was a woman, the managing editor was a woman (I was her assistant), the secretaries and assistants all were women. The head of anything was a man.

Men at Popular Library worked their way not up but sideways. Actually it turned out that very few men really work their way up from the mailroom; all the department heads were once salesmen. And since traveling salesmen traditionally are male, there wasn't much chance for a woman.

To top it off, Popular Library published very little science fiction. The editor-in-chief didn't seem very fond of it, and he was quite happy to foist off on me—the resident expert on weird—anything that was strange. He wasn't the only one. The acquisitions editor once dragged me to a screening of a low budget science fiction/horror film because *I* was to make the decision for or against a novelized tie-in.

Not too many women admitted to reading science fiction, which was still thought of as being for men. But when I left Popular Library and went to Ballantine Books, I discovered that Betty Ballantine had been buying science fiction and fantasy for years. Of course, Betty was married to the company's owner and could do what she wanted. Still, if the books weren't selling, Ian Ballantine would not have continued to publish them.

My years at Ballantine were not only instructive but practical. My editor-in-chief for Ballantine's lesser imprints—Beagle and Boxer books—was Donald R. Bensen. Don had been in publishing for a long time; he'd been an acquisitions editor and an editor-in-chief before, and he introduced me to all sorts of devious ways to get things done—in addition to doing everything myself. . . .

Since publishers were—and still are—cheap, the entire Beagle/Boxer staff consisted of Don, me, one full-time secretary, and an occasional file clerk. Together we put out ten titles a month. I functioned as editor and copywriter as well as promotion, publicity, and advertising director. Beagle was the women's line; it consisted mainly of romances. Boxer, the "male" line of books, published mysteries, adventure, and science fiction. How typical.

A mystery buff, Don was also a science fiction/fantasy/horror fan. He was responsible for bringing H. P. Lovecraft back into print after many years; several Lovecraft titles appeared under the Boxer imprint and Ballantine later reprinted them with fancy, new, and horrific covers. By then, Lovecraft had really caught on and the books sold better than ever.

Through Don, and Ballantine, I met an ever-widening circle of writers in the genre. Lin Carter was a consulting fantasy editor, and I remember one memorable day when Lin dropped by, bringing along L. Sprague de Camp. I had never met Sprague—didn't know him at all. But when he found out I was a fan, he proceeded to act out a scene from one of his books, complete with dialect and gestures. It made quite an impression on me. After all, here I was, a nobody, struggling with five jobs at once in a tiny office made of two walls and a partition, without power and recognition (let alone a raise in salary), and I had a box-office seat to a personal live performance by a famous author.

This was the early seventies. Up until this point, the science fiction editor usually got the job by default. The editor-in-chief (someone not familiar with the genre but who knew it sold books), during a round-table editorial meeting, would point to some hapless male editor and say, "You! You're only doing two Westerns and a War book, you can edit science fiction too." Or, with the influx of so many female employees and editors, that line sometimes got changed to: "You, the dumb blonde on the end, you're overpaid and underworked, *you* can edit science fiction."

Neither assumption was nice nor accurate. Men and dumb blondes do not make good science-fiction editors unless they have read extensively in the field and understand what science fiction and fantasy really is. (Of course I can't explain it to you or to publishers, it's something that has to be learned.)

Furthermore, science fiction has always been a steady money-maker. When the editor understands the field and buys the appropriate books, the books continue to sell. When the publisher puts a true dumb blonde in charge, the books bomb. Proof of this was my next job. . . .

Although I loved working for Don Bensen, things at Ballantine were getting hairy. The company was sold to Random House and whole departments suddenly disappeared. As the months went by, we had weekly going-away parties. Being fired was preferable to quitting, because of unemployment compensation. I remember one employee who was so thrilled to be fired that when she left her good-bye cake said "Congratulations."

Meanwhile, Boxer Books had disappeared; since they rivaled the regular Ballantine list, they were absorbed. Don Bensen became part of the Ballantine editorial staff and I was left to take care of the romances. I was less than thrilled, especially when one morning Don announced that the powers-that-be were holding a special meeting to decide the fate of Beagle Books. I had not been invited. Not only were female employees with no real power expendable, we were invisible. Before I could crash the meeting (something that feminine lil ol' me was determined to do), Don came by again to announce we'd been reprieved. Someone had finally bothered to look at the sale figures. . . .

After that, I resolved to work elsewhere. Betty Ballantine had already left the company and was replaced by Judy-Lynn del Rey, who came from *Galaxy* magazine. Aside from Betty Ballantine, Judy-Lynn was the only female science fiction editor I knew about—and I wanted to be one too! When Judy-Lynn heard that Doubleday was looking for an editor, she recommended me.

Doubleday is one of the few hardcover companies that actively publish science fiction and fantasy and has continued to do so since the 1950s. Their list contains the most illustrious names in the field. And they were one of the very few publishers who had a special position just for a science fiction editor who did that and nothing else.

So I "auditioned" for the Doubleday brass. Though I desperately wanted the job, there were a few things I could not disguise. Myself, for instance.

I tried to dress conservatively; at least I think my clothes matched. But my résumé was something else. Not only did it list all the publishers I worked for before—including the defunct newspaper and *Foreign Affairs Quarterly* where I worked in the Fulfillment Department—but it also listed my previous careers which ran the gamut from window decorator to medical secretary (where I got ptomaine poisoning in the hospital cafeteria).

My tackiness appealed to department head Larry Ashmead, who also recommended me. If I passed muster with the brass, I could have the job. And so I found myself being ushered through the hallowed Doubleday halls by the managing editor who introduced me to all sorts of people—so many people, in fact, that I forgot to whom I was being introduced. I came at last to a tall, genial man who shook my hand, looked at my checkered résumé, and asked, "Tell me, what have you learned from working at so many publishers?"

"Well," I said earnestly, "it makes me wonder how some people get to be presidents of publishing companies!"

Guess who I was talking to. . . .

Fortunately, Doubleday president Sam Vaughan laughed uproariously and hired me. And Doubleday is where I honed my skills as an acquisitions editor. They dearly loved publishing science fiction, but they didn't want to pay much money for it. I could buy any manuscript I liked, as long as it didn't cost more than $3,000. In addition, a book had to be exactly 192 pages long and contain no four letter words.

This was based on the special way Doubleday sold their books—by a subscription system—to schools and libraries. The books could be guaranteed to make money as long as the formula was followed exactly. So it was here that I learned another publishing axiom: pay as little as possible to an author. The corollary is: after you've paid the author virtually no money, make sure the publisher owns all rights.

After all, this is really an editor's job. Although the editor is the buffer between an author and the powers-that-be, an editor is charged with finding a "property"—be it an author or a book—that will make a profit.

Since the subscription system meant I could take a chance on new writers, I actively read through what is euphemistically known as "the slush pile." The slush is anything sent to a publisher that the publisher didn't know was coming: all the manuscripts from would-be writers from Oshkosh to Hoboken. In fact, anything remotely resembling science fiction was shipped en masse, from every department, to my desk.

In desperation, I prepared a photocopied rejection letter which listed all the reasons (check one or more) why I and the company were not interested in a particular submission. Some were quite simple and reasonable: We don't publish short story collections by unknown writers. Others were all the "Out" topics that non-science fiction readers thought were "In": Utopia; Atlantis; World War III; Jesus is an alien from Mars, or Venus, or Alpha Centaurii (check one or more); anything resembling a Grade-B horror movie; anything that began, "Beam me up, Scotty". . . .

The slush has existed for generations, though in earlier times it was referred to as "over the transom" material. This dates back to when would-be writers were not allowed into a publisher's office. The desperate writers would literally shove a manuscript through the open transom section at the top of the closed office door. It would hit with a thud and then the publisher was stuck with it. . . .

While at Doubleday, I discovered some wonderful people in the slush pile: John Crowley, winner of the World Fantasy Award and nominated for The American Book Awards; Eric van Lustbader, author of the best-selling *The Ninja*; Octavia Butler, one of the few black women writing in the field. I also continued to publish and promote authors such as Charles L. Grant, starting his acclaimed and award-winning anthology series *Shadows*, Stuart D. Schiff, publisher of *Whispers*, a small quality magazine devoted to fantasy and horror, and Geo. Alec Effinger, whose whimsical fantasy and black humor is such a delight.

There were so many authors—in science fiction, fantasy and horror— whom I now knew on a first-name basis, that for the three years I ran Doubleday's science fiction line, I was in sheer heaven.

But I've been off on a pleasant tangent. I want to get back to dumb blondes. Although the previous editor at Doubleday was dedicated and hard-working, she knew very little about the field. As a consequence, many of the books and authors she chose to publish did not fare well; many were not picked up by the paperback publishers for reprint. Since a hardcover house needs that subsidiary rights money, the situation had to change. Once I started buying books that were true to the genre, the reprint sales picked up dramatically. Of course, science fiction was also in a boom cycle from 1974 to 1977, but it helped that Doubleday had the product to fill the demand.

While riding high at Doubleday, an old friend from Popular Library days, Bob Gleason, called and offered me a position at Playboy Books, where he was now editor-in-chief. This leads to another old publishing axiom—and which applies to Hollywood too: friends in high places are good to have. Playboy Books was both hardcover and paperback, and they published all sorts of things from thrillers to historical romances to nonfiction. They would also pay lots more money than Doubleday, so I packed my bags.

Doubleday asked me to recommend a replacement, having learned not to hire dumb blondes, and I suggested Pat LoBrutto. (It was Pat who'd worked his way up from the mailroom at Ace.)

About a year after going to Playboy, under the direction of the general manager and with the support of the editor-in-chief, I was asked to start a separate science-fiction line. The general manager, rightly so, had decided there was money to be made.

I operated similarly to the way I had at Doubleday: with a fairly free rein. I bought what I liked, though sometimes, during an editorial meeting, when I struggled to explain a particularly bizarre novel, I could see the rest of the staff was either left at the gate or laughing hysterically.

I also had much greater control over the book covers. Back at Doubleday, I worked with an art director who had little money and less imagination, favoring collages for the hardcover book covers. I remember one Frederik Pohl cover which showed Fred with a pencil for his head. But in paperback publishing, the cover is the most important element of bookselling. A cover can make or break a book. Since the Playboy art director was more than willing to listen to my suggestions, I could exercise what I had learned at Don Wollheim's knee.

Generalities, however, can backfire. One day the general manager came back from a trip to Dalton headquarters. B. Dalton's is one of the country's leading bookstore chains; when they order a book, they order it in the thousands. That week, the computer at Dalton's, which kept track of sales, showed that science-fiction books with spaceships on the cover sold the best. So the general manager was determined to put spaceships on the covers of all our books, whether or not the books had any spaceships in them.

One of the many things I accomplished at Playboy was to put sex back into science fiction.

I had been interested in sex for a long time. In science fiction, that is. Books in the field had gone through cycles, and I thought it was again time to add spice to the stories. I couldn't do it at Doubleday because of their subscription system, but I could certainly do it at Playboy. (I had already put up with jokes from my authors about editing in a tail and ears.) So I let it be known that I was looking for sexy science fiction.

Some of the submissions I received cannot be repeated here, but one of my favorites was *Samantha Spade and the Pansy-Lesbo Outer-Space Caper*, in which galactic detective Samantha Spade spent the entire first chapter answering her video-phone in the nude. Instead of getting science fiction with sex, I was being sent futuristic pornography. After a very long search, two things happened: an agent sent me some underground classics by Philip José Farmer and I decided to create a sexy science fiction series from scratch.

First, with the novels by Phil Farmer, I bought up all that were available. These were science fictional stories with fantastic elements that delved deeply into the psychology and sociology of sex. They had been published years ago by a small, very unusual company, and no one had been willing to touch them since, despite Farmer's name. British editions of the books were being bootlegged under the table at five dollars a paperback, so I knew I had a winner, and the Playboy editions of the Farmer books sold like proverbial hot cakes.

But there were very few properties around like those Farmer books; the final solution was to create a new series. In the interim, the general manager had asked me to analyze *Heavy Metal* magazine in order to figure out what made it popular. Perhaps we could use those elements in the new series. The magazine, however, had virtually no words: it was visually oriented, bizarre, sexy, and made no sense to me. However, I forged ahead and cast about for a likely author, one who knew not only science fiction and fantasy, but who could write sex scenes. I settled on Andrew J. Offutt, an experienced writer who had written in many genres, including pornography, and we had a very long lunch, hammering out what would go into making a successful series. I had wanted something that would combine the thrills of *Star Wars*, the warmth of *Star Trek*, and the bizarreness of *Heavy Metal*. The result was *Spaceways*: High Adventure for Adults. . . .

It had pirates, freebooters, slaves, bordellos, blasters, scantily clad girls, macho men, aliens, and just about everything else we could think of. To launch the series with a bang (no pun intended), I wanted a title for the first book in the series that would turn heads. So I called it *Of Alien Bondage*. So far, I think there are about seventeen books in the *Spaceways* series, which has about run its course by now. But those books, along with some of the other unusual titles I published at Playboy, began a new trend.

If I had been a true dumb blonde, working for a publisher looking to cut corners, then the books I edited would not have been successful. However, it was only after a number of years in the field during which time both I and the publishers grew in knowledge, that things worked. When I was finally in charge it was because the publishers wanted me in charge and because I could deliver.

Nowadays, when I go to conventions and gatherings, I find that a lot of people have heard my name. The science-fiction community is large and varied, almost like an extended family, but I'm always surprised to find myself a minor celebrity, hobnobbing with the very writers whose books I idolized.

Not bad for a dumb blonde, even if I am a brunette. . . .

I'll never forget Lloyd Biggle's shoes.

It was our first meeting and he'd come all the way from Michigan to see me, his New York editor. He walked in the door, hand outstretched. I got a fleeting impression of dark hair, round face, blue pants, plaid jacket—and my gaze traveled down to his feet and stayed firmly rooted there, like Crazy Glue. Lloyd wore white shoes like the kind of white bucks I used to wear in high school.

We shook hands, chatted—and all the while I could not tear my eyes from his white shoes. Eventually my attention finally settled on his cherubic face and we got down to business. But after all these years, I can't help but think of Lloyd's shoes each time I see him. (What makes this meeting even more interesting is that Lloyd swears he never owned any white shoes. . . .)

Back then, Lloyd was being regularly published by Doubleday; he had a continuing series featuring an intergalactic trouble-shooter named Jan Darzek. Lloyd is also the author of some fifteen science-fiction books, including such classics as *Monument, All the Colors of Darkness*, and *The Still, Small Voice of Trumpets*. His numerous short stories have appeared just about everywhere you could name.

His essay was adapted from a speech delivered to a conference of science-fiction teachers held at Eastern Michigan University. Though Lloyd left the academic field many years ago, he has maintained close contacts with it, and his special interest is the use of science fiction in schools and colleges. Down through the years he has been bemused and appalled by the attitude toward science fiction held by many academics, critics and literary historians. Unfortunately, this didactic is on a question that has yet to be resolved: Just what the heck is science fiction, anyway? Lloyd's suggested answer is quite unusual. . . .

9

ROOTS: A TAXICAB TOUR OF SCIENCE-FICTION HISTORY

LLOYD BIGGLE, JR.

The first interplanetary romance, science-fiction historians will tell you, was created in the second century by a writer known to history as Lucian the Scoffer. The characters in his story sailed beyond the Pillars of Hercules into the Western Ocean, and a waterspout picked them up and landed them on the moon.

The historians are wrong.

Humans began to wonder about the moon very early in their conscious existence. I have no historical evidence to support that statement, but I feel confident in asserting that the moon is such a conspicuous object in the night sky that our primitive ancestors must have noticed it and wondered what it was or what they would experience if they went there. The first interplanetary romance was born many thousands of years before Lucian when a tribe gathered at night on an African hilltop to look at the moon and listen raptly while an archetypal sage, or bard, or witch doctor spun tales about it.

That was the first interplanetary romance but not the first science fiction. And what is science fiction?

In 1952, in a review column in the magazine *Science Fiction Adventures*, Damon Knight published a credo for critics of science fiction in which he described the futility of attempting to define it. He called the term a misnomer that we are stuck with and declared that it will do us no particular harm if we remember that it means what we point to when we say it. A few years ago I told him that this 1952 definition still seemed to me to be the most useful one that I had encountered, and he said, "Well, yes—but people are pointing to such *strange* things these days."

Attempts to define "science fiction" remind me of the fable of the blind men and the elephant. For those whose culturally impoverished childhoods did not include fables, that one describes an encounter with an elephant by three blind men. One embraced the animal's leg and thought it very like a tree trunk. Another caught hold of the tall and vehemently disagreed; the evidence of his own hands proved that the elephant was like a rope. The third explored the elephant's side and pronounced it to be like a wall. They went their way arguing, and none of them was able to convince the others.

Definers of science fiction use the same selective technique. I will make no attempt to couch this essay in terms that will cover everything that has crept under the science-fiction tent since World War II. Science fiction is what I point to when I say it, and I am pointing a long way back in time.

The word "science" has connotations of knowledge, factual information, and precise, verifiable experiments. The word "fiction" refers to the feigned, the imagined, and the fabricated. When we put them together to form a term, science fiction, the literal meaning would be true-false literature. The first thing any student of science fiction should understand is that the term is logically a monstrosity and historically an accident. Not only was there science fiction long before anyone thought of calling it that; there was science fiction long before anyone recognized the existence of either science or fiction.

Contemporary science fiction is a modern manifestation of an extremely old branch of literature—perhaps the oldest. It has deep roots in ancient myths and folklore. It is a reflection of humanity's eternal quest for the unknown, and it derives from two of the most fundamental of human drives: Humanity always has produced its dreamers who wonder and speculated about the beyond; and its seekers and adventurers who had to go there and find out. Mount Everest was climbed because it was there. The same quality of aspiration will land humans on Mars whenever that becomes possible. There will be lengthy discussions of the scientific benefits to accrue from such a journey, but, in the end, the trip will be made because Mars is there. If interplanetary space vehicles could be built in back yards, the first Martian explorers would have left long ago.

Today our challenge is the solar system. Primitive humans, inhabiting a world where every faint breeze was a question mark and each flash of lightning a stroke of doom, faced different challenges—some trivial to us but all appallingly formidable to them: what lay beyond the mountain, or across the sea, or—remember that forty thousand years ago Neanderthal man buried his dead with weapons and tools—what they would encounter beyond life.

When humanity wonders and, for a moment or a millennium, is unable to find out, the other basic human urge takes over: the urge to speculate, to invent, to dream. When our primitive ancestors were unable to learn firsthand what was beyond the mountain, or across the sea, or beyond life, there was a dreamer in their tribe who could tell them. Some of the dreamers became professionals and even managed to make a living at it. They were the witch doctors, or the medicine men, or the priests. We still have such professional dreamers, though in this rational age most of them preface their dreams with "maybe" or "might" or "on the other hand, if." Or they may frankly call their dreams fiction. In fact, science fiction. As with their primitive forerunners, modern professional science-fiction authors think dreaming is a lot more fun than hunting the woolly mammoth for a living.

If you think it is safer, though, you have never attended a science-fiction convention.

Down through the millennia, the literature we are calling science fiction has satisfied humanity's persistent quest for an understanding of the unknown: Yesterday, what lay beyond the mountain; today, the solar system; tomorrow, the universe; even that strangest, most challenging universe of all, the human mind. Humanity always has been its own greatest mystery, its most challenging unknown, and with the blank spaces on the map of the Earth filled in, it should not be surprising that a foremost concern of today's science-fiction writers is humanity itself.

But only yesterday, or the day before, the most challenging mystery was the far shore of the Mediterranean Sea, and one of the greatest science fiction writers of all time, Homer, filled in that blank with his epic account of the wanderings of Ulysses. This is the classic statement of one of the great themes of literature, the fantastic journey, a theme that was already venerable when Homer used it in the ninth century B.C. It has remained a mainstay of literature right down to the present, because whenever we shatter a dream by going there and finding out for ourselves, we always discover a new horizon to wonder about—just as our primitive ancestors, when they finally ventured to see for themselves what lay beyond the mountain, found another mountain.

Think of Ulysses, think of Sinbad the Sailor, think of Gulliver, Robinson Crusoe, and the entire vast panorama of fantastic literary journeys right down to the relatively recent fantastic voyage through the human bloodstream. No wonder that when Marco Polo returned to Italy, he was dismissed as only another dreamer, a writer of science fiction. There had been so many dreamers of fantastic journeys before him.

These dreams out of the past assuredly are science fiction, but literary historians do not recognize them as such. Why not? Because science fiction dates. It becomes dated.

Consider this example: In 1873, Jules Verne published a classic science-fiction novel entitled, *Around the World in Eighty Days*. It presented a notion that was truly fantastic at the time, and Verne described its events with the same order of believable detail that modern science-fiction writers lavish on tales of journeys to other worlds. The novel turns on a scientific fact—that when one travels completely around the Earth, one gains or loses an entire day depending on the direction traveled. The public had very little reason to be familiar with this fact in 1873, a date when global travelers were few in number. This may be difficult to comprehend at a time when everyone has a tale to tell of jet fatigue or time lag. In 1873, *Around the World in Eighty Days* was exciting, colorful science fiction, even though the term had not been invented. Today, when artificial satellites circle the earth in a few hours, *Around the World in Eighty Days* is a quaint historical romance. It does not seem like science fiction. It has become dated.

In the same way, the journey to the moon was yesterday's science fiction; it is today's realistic adventure; and it will be tomorrow's history. Many science-fiction classics of other eras are not recognizable as science fiction. For critics and literary historians, the difficulty is compounded by the fact that the term *science fiction* was not invented until well into the twentieth century. Perhaps it is unfair to expect them to recognize a science fiction classic when its title page does not bear the legend, *A Sci-*

ence Fiction Novel. (Even a contemporary work of science fiction may not be recognized as such if it lacks that label.)

Critics of ancient times did not base their judgments on literary labels, and they treated science-fiction writers more kindly. Neither Longinus nor Aristotle blasted Homer for writing trashy, unbelievable fantasy stuffed with religious miracles and unhuman monsters from remote islands. (Modern translation: scientific miracles and unhuman aliens from remote worlds.)

Journeys to distant parts of the Earth are now made so routinely that the modern reader has difficulty in perceiving those earlier journeys as the stuff of daring imaginative speculation. Equally confusing to critics and historians is the fact that most of those early journeys are made by water, in sailing ships called galleys, or triremes, or galleons, or frigates. The fantastic journey to another world or another galaxy is necessarily made by spaceship. The literary difference is obvious, isn't it? If there is a spaceship, it is science fiction. If there isn't, it isn't.

What this means is that our literary critics and historians are classifying literature according to what I call the "taxicab method." The literary type that a story or novel belongs to is determined by the mode of transportation used by its characters. If the characters in a novel arrive in a strange land by sailing ship, this is satire, or Utopian romance, or whatever the historian chances to decide upon. In another novel, exactly the same kind of story, the characters arrive in a strange land by spaceship, and that automatically is science fiction.

Literary historians of course have every right to set their own parameters, but we have the right to insist that they apply those parameters consistently. Carried to its logical conclusion, the taxicab method becomes an invaluable tool for the delineation of literary subtypes. If a character drives his own car, that is one kind of literature. If he goes by bus, that is another. When, inevitably, the forces of purity exert their influence, writers will be forbidden to mix two literary subtypes in the same story. If the characters go by bus in chapter 1, sending them by subway in chapter 2 would constitute an inexcusable sabotage of an established literary principle.

The striking advantages of the taxicab method are that it is simple, it is obvious, and it can be applied without thinking. What modern literary critics and historians need more than anything else is a classification method that can be applied without thinking. In fact, that is the approach to science fiction that they have always used.

The fantastic journey is one of the many themes of today's science fiction that have venerable histories. The concept of a lost island, or a lost civilization, or a lost continent must have been old when Plato described Atlantis. More recent examples have been Arthur Conan Doyle's *The Lost World*; James Hilton's *Lost Horizon*—which gave our language a new word, Shangri-La; Kipling's *The Man Who Would be King; The Valley of the Blind*, by H. G. Wells—the list can be a long, long one. These titles are not generally known as science fiction. The taxicab method is responsible for that. The story of a civilization discovered in the chasms of Mars, as in C. S. Lewis's *Out of the Silent Planet*, involves a spaceship, so that indubitably is science fiction. The story of an unknown civilization discovered in the Himalayas is not. Shangri-La was reached by airplane (but the characters had to walk back). There is, as yet, no special literary subtype for stories with characters who walk part way. Perhaps this is fortunate. Walking back poses almost insurmountable difficulties for the characters in an interplanetary romance.

Sometimes these remote or lost civilizations are called Utopias after the famous work by Sir Thomas More. This theme also goes back to ancient Greece and beyond. Plato's *Republic* was an early example, and the Utopian theme is still popular in present-day science fiction. A modern contribution is to turn the theme inside out: Instead of describing the most desirable of societies, the author creates the most undesirable—a dystopia or cacotopia that demonstrates what could happen here and now if humanity doesn't straighten itself out. Huxley's *Brave New World* is a dystopian novel, as is Orwell's *1984*. Utopian literature, positive or negative, is not commonly called science fiction, but all of it is. Unfortunately, Utopias are set in distant places in space or time and must be reached by some kind of journey. This permits our critics and historians to classify them by the taxicab method. For example, Sir Francis Bacon's *New Atlantis* was discovered by sailing ship, which of course prevents it from being science fiction.

I want to make very clear this unbroken continuity of science-fiction themes from early times right down to the present. Here is an extremely common science-fiction situation: A spaceship crashes on a strange planet. All of the crew are killed except one, and this one man engages in a heroic struggle to survive in a strange and perilous environment. He holds out for years, vainly awaiting rescue, and then one day, on one of his forays, he discovers—a human footprint!

Spaceman Robinson Crusoe, of course.

Or supposing that when he arrives on this strange planet, he falls asleep and awakes to find that he has been tied up by little men. He would become a spaceman Gulliver—which would be unfortunate, because *Gulliver's Travels* do not need updating. They are in one of the all-time science-fiction classics, and they beautifully typify the fantastic journey theme: Shipwreck or capture by pirates or whatever; the lost or unknown civilization described—in this case, with tongue firmly in cheek; and the return home. Science fiction, whether the journey is by sailing ship or spaceship.

Notice how easily these classic plots slide up and down the centuries. L. Sprague de Camp has demonstrated how the *Beowolf* plot, an eighth century epic, can be converted into a tale of the future by changing the ship to a spaceship and adding a little hardware.

The robot, or android, with its computerized positronic brain and magnetic memory tapes, would seem to be a thoroughly modern invention. It is not. It is as old as mythology. There was Talos, the brazen robot built for King Minos of Crete. There were myths of gods attended by handmaidens made of gold and of statues that came alive and moved from place to place and spoke. Don't forget Pygmalion, King of Cyprus, who made an ivory statue and fell in love with it—whereupon Aphrodite brought it to life. The history of robots, both in fact and in fiction, is fascinating. The achievements of ancient technology were remarkable, but contemporary achievements of the human imagination always have outstripped technology by far. *We don't have to be able to build the hardware in order to create things in our imaginations.*

The culmination of the literary development of the robot did not come with today's computers. It happened back in 1818, when Mary Shelley's unfortunate young scientist Frankenstein succeeded in building the ultimate robot—one that was actually alive. Whenever I read a newspaper story about the most recent heart transplant, I think of Mary Shelley's Frankenstein poking about in dissecting rooms and cemeteries looking for spare parts, and I reflect that she anticipated all of that. She also anticipated what has been facetiously described as the typical science-fiction love story: Boy meets girl; boy loses girl; boy *builds* girl.

I already have mentioned the venerability of tales of other worlds. The first *recorded* space platform was launched by Aristophanes in his play, *The Birds*, back in 414 B.C. He called it "Cloudcuckooland." As with the robots, primitive humans did not have to build the hardware in order to circle the Earth or travel to the moon in their imaginations.

Throughout human history, every age has produced a "science fiction" that reflects its own technology and scientific thought: a science fiction that is the realization of its own understanding of the universe. At any time in history, the human imagination could fly to the moon. If the author described the trip as a narrative, so that he had to account logically for his physical presence on the moon by explaining how he got there, the mode of transportation that he chose depended on the technology of the age in which the story was created, from feathers glued onto the arms to make wings right up to—as early as the seventeenth century—rockets. If you know your military history, you will know that rockets were a major military weapon in the seventeenth and eighteenth centuries. That is how the "rockets' red glare" got into our national anthem.

This can be illustrated in another way with a science fiction theme that is comparatively modern: time travel.

The first known example has been found in an obscure story published in England in 1842. Only a year later came *A Christmas Carol*, by Charles Dickens, with its Spirits of Christmas Past, Present, and Future. Next came a famous Utopian work, Edward Bellamy's *Looking Backward*. Bellamy's Utopia was located in the future, which gave him a different kind of transportation problem from that of authors who populated fictitious islands with their Utopias. The next prominent example was *A Connecticut Yankee in King Arthur's Court*, by Mark Twain. Finally, in 1895, came *The Time Machine*, by H. G. Wells.

Characters move through time in all of these works, but the different techniques employed by the authors to effect that movement make a fascinating study. Dickens used ghosts or spirits to waft his characters through time. Mark Twain used a rap on the head. Bellamy's character took a sleeping pill and woke up a hundred and thirteen years later (I would strongly advise that would-be writers should not try that on a modern science-fiction editor). All of these works represent rather primitive technologies of time travel; but H. G. Wells was caught up in that wonderful outburst of science and technology at the end of the nineteenth century, when it was thought that human ingenuity could construct anything and that science and technology would in short order solve all human problems, and H. G. Wells's character *built* a time machine.

But look carefully at what he built. The novels contains very little description of the machine, but the character is clearly shown seated on the saddle of a contrivance like a bicycle or a motorcycle. H. G. Wells invented a fantastically futuresque device, but he described it in terms of late nineteenth-century-technology.

When this profound science-fiction principle first occurred to me, I picked up a book of my own about time travel—the novel, *The Fury out of Time*, which was first published in 1965. I found to my considerable amusement that my time-travel device was the spitting image of an artificial satellite.

The science fiction of every age reflects its own technology and scientific thought, and that, of course, is the principal reason that science fiction dates. The far-fetched and the futuresque in one age seems old fashioned to another and is not recognized as science fiction.

Please note that the taxicab method of literary classification operates with a vengeance on time-travel stories. If an author has his character travel through time by oversleeping, as Bellamy did, or if he propels him through time with a knock on the head, as Mark Twain did, that is literature. If the character builds a *machine* that travels through time, that is science fiction. Once again it is the mode of transportation that determines the literary type.

The journey plays two roles in literature. In one of them, it is an end in itself. The *Odyssey* is a series of marvelous adventures, but once the problem of Ulysses's homecoming is resolved, the story is over.

In contrast to this "getting there is all the fun" kind of story, the more common use of the journey is to move the characters—and the reader—to the place where the story is going to occur; the quicker, the better. This usually limits the journey to an opening chapter or section, with a possible return journey glossed over in the final chapter. In an attempt to supply a logical basis for such devices as time travel or faster-than-light travel, authors sometimes construct long, profoundly abstruse introductions that explain far more than the reader wants to know. Either a reader accepts the fact that one can fall down a rabbit hole and find a strange civilization, or the reader doesn't. And if the reader doesn't, probably he wouldn't find Lewis Carroll any more convincing if *Alice in Wonderland* had begun with a lengthy chapter on: rabbit holes, past, present and future; mysterious variations in their depths and dimensions; the effect of various types of soils on rabbit holes; myths and legends connected with rabbit holes; and various rabbit holes the author had known personally. Instead, Carroll set the scene in two short paragraphs, at the end of which he already had introduced the rabbit.

The point I am making here is that the taxicab method of literary classification sets apart works with a spaceship or a time machine even when the only role played by these props is the exact equivalent of Alice's tumble down the rabbit hole. Their function is to move the characters, and the reader, to the place where the story is going to happen.

Another venerable theme still found in various guises in today's science fiction is the mad (or elderly) scientist. He is at least as old as Aristophanes's play, *The Clouds*, where the eccentric professor was a caricature of the philosopher Socrates. I don't know what unsung genius first gave that mad scientist a beautiful daughter, but whoever did it fully deserves his own literary monument.

If science-fiction's bug-eyed monsters impress you as demented creations of a contemporary pseudobiology, ask yourself whether you would enjoy meeting this one: "His serpent's body is as strong as an enraged bull. He has a human face; but instead of a nose he has the beak of an eagle. He possesses a goose's eyes, an ass's ears, and the teeth of a dog. His tongue is long and venomous; with which, when he is chafed, he darts a prodigious number of fire-brands united with a smoke so fetid, that it is enough to infect a whole city. He has the legs, feet, and claws of a lion; a dragon's tail, which is as long as a lance. His back is armed with a scale so hard, that no steel, however excellently tempered, is able to penetrate. Morever, the shoulders are ornamented with the strong wings of a Griffin, which enable him to cleave the air with tremendous rapidity."

This is a creature called a "Grippe" as described in a medieval French manuscript. (I ask you to note that this medieval description of a fictitious monster reflects that age's view of biology, just as stories about moon travel or time travel reflect an age's technology.) I personally would rather take my chances with science-fiction's bug-eyed monsters. Some of them really are quite nice.

If, despite all of this evidence of venerable themes, you still see striking differences in modern science fiction, you are entirely correct. The large roles that science and technology play in modern science fiction do not count as differences, however. These only reflect the fact that we live in a scientific and technological age. As I have pointed out, the science fiction of every age reflects contemporary science and technology.

There are two highly significant differences: modern science fiction's attitude toward the future, and its realistic treatment of space travel and remote worlds. We of the twentieth century may have difficulty in comprehending that there was a time when only seers and scholars had any real concept of change in human affairs. Not until the industrial revolution accelerated change and made it seem to occur at a measurable rate was it considered possible to *calculate* the future. The modern seer eschews tea leaves, trances, and the entrails of animals to reach for his computer—though the number of calculations that turn out to be miscalculations suggests that humanity might be better served if its seers occasionally resorted to tea leaves.

Outer space and the future—singly or in combination—are modern science fiction's home territory. Science fiction is sometimes criticized for presenting views that are "larger than life." This is as true as it is inevitable because everything "out there" is projected and magnified. Earth's problems, compared with those of the galaxy, are the problems of a rural political ward compared with a life-or-death crisis at the United Nations. Humanity's capacity for villainy is tremendously magnified in outer space. So is its scope for heroism.

Remember the flight of Apollo 13? Compared with your automobile, a spacecraft is unbelievably flimsy. If you read science fiction, you know that the one thing the astronauts positively could not do was slam on the brakes, turn around, and come back—400,000 miles from home in a flimsy craft, and no one within radio distance who could possibly make a service call, and the damned thing blew up under them. Do you remember the first message after the explosion? "Okay, Houston, we have a problem."

Outer space is the ultimate destination of science fiction because it is humanity's ultimate destination. There will be giants out there; there already have been.

By projecting the problems of here and now across the space frontier, we can magnify them and see them more clearly, and we can achieve understanding where it is denied to us when we view the events from close by. Some problems—artificial problems—disappear when projected into outer space. The problem of race is almost nonexistent in science fiction. As L. Sprague de Camp once pointed out, when one has been contemplating the problem of relations with the Sirian Spider Men, no human being can seem alien.

In summary: The bases for the science fiction of all ages are humanity's quest for the unknown and its superb talent for imaginative dreaming. In the past two thousand years, those qualities of human aspiration have led mankind to explore a world and discover two universes—one in the sky and the other in its own mind. Beyond those universes may lie only other universes, just as primitive humans found only mountains beyond mountains, but as long as there is an unknown, anywhere, to wonder about, humanity will continue to dream science fiction.

Apart from its mundane values, be they literary, scientific, or whatever, science fiction has much to teach us concerning ourselves. We project against the universe our joys and sorrows, our bravery and cowardice, our love and hatred, our selfishness and greed and meanness and nobility and generosity, our cruelty and our kindness—and thereby we take humanity's ultimate measurement.

I think it was nearly ten years ago when I first met Geo. Alec Effinger. Previously, I had only corresponded with him, and now he was in town, all set to visit his editor—me. I casually mentioned this to the editor next door, and she said, "Oh, you mean Piglet is coming."

"Piglet!" I thought, horrified. "What kind of name is that for a human being?"

I mean, I knew that science-fiction writers were unusual, but just how unusual could this one be? I had visions of a huge, fat, pink, hairless thing, wearing a turtleneck and tweeds, paying a call. I contemplated being out when he arrived.

But having a strong sense of duty, I remained at my desk and was ready for George's visit. In came a short, thin, perfectly ordinary guy wearing a black turtleneck sweater and jeans. He was bright, friendly, winsome, and endearing. And he had hair. In fact, he made me want to pat him on the head and feed him chicken soup (not something I'd do for a porker).

By the time I'd met George, his first novel was in print (*What Entropy Means to Me*) and he'd had numerous short stories published. This body of work had already garnered him a nomination for the John W. Campbell Award for Best New Writer. He's had a short story appear in nearly every magazine that has existed since 1970, from *Vertex* to *Fantasy & Science Fiction* to *Isaac Asimov's SF Magazine*. To date he's had about eight novels and four short-story collections published, and his latest novels, *The Bird of Time* and *Saving Time* will be brought out by his major publisher, Doubleday & Co. Nearly everything he has written is speculative fiction, which is another term often used for unclassifiable science fiction. . . .

George's works often defy description, but they usually have one unifying element: humor. In fact he wants the authors of *The Science Fiction Book of Lists* to know that he is perturbed at not making their Humorous List and having his name in lights up there with Ron Goulart's. As George puts it, he writes "funny stuff."

He has even managed to write funny stuff about some depressing subjects, as you will see in his very special essay.

10
WRITING THROUGH ADVERSITY
GEO. ALEC EFFINGER

When Sharon Jarvis, my dear friend and editor, suggested that I contribute an essay to this collection, I was flattered and immediately excited. I suggested a topic I felt I could explore with fresh insight, and that was "Humor in Science Fiction." Sharon's reaction, as I recall, was, "Uh, maybe." She had another subject in mind for me all the time: "Writing through Adversity." Now, giving somebody a line like that is like dressing a kid up as a monster from *Alien* and sending him out trick-or-treating for UNICEF on April 15th. Nobody wants to go on about despair and how it might affect the delicate workings of the creative process. It's a cheerless subject pretty obviously, and writing about it is destined to be kind of a thankless task. Anybody who tackled this kind of stuff was going to look like one of those abject winners on *Queen for a Day*, holding a dozen long-stemmed American Beauty roses and almost enough money for her mother's iron lung machine.

So I will not talk about despair.

At this point, I'm not even sure how near I'm going to edge toward adversity, although, *believe me*, what I don't know about adversity—

—I'll probably learn next week. But we all know adversity, don't we, chaps? I mean, we've all had our share of slings and arrows. There is some serious thought that holds with the idea that adversity is what sparks expression in an artist; that a similarly talented person who never faced such adversity might never find the need for such expression. But the hell with serious thought, I say. What I'm going to do is go on for a while about how certain types of adversity are easier to cope with, given the writer's life; and how other types can be more than normally aggravating. And I will be lighthearted about the whole matter, so you won't even notice that you're reading about gloom and desperation and such things. I will write the essay, but I will do it my own way, and the only way to make such a compromise is to forget at the outset that there ever was such a thing as good taste. If you want *tasteful* despair, they have Russian novelists for that. I work the other side of the street entirely, buddy.

But where to start, where to start? I remember standing on the street corner at the age of ten—this is Cleveland, Ohio, yet—the snow swirling madly around my red and stinging ears, my unmittened hands holding a stack of sodden newspapers. A long black car pulled to a stop beside me, in the thick, wet slush. From the back seat, a sinewy, gaunt hand rolled down the window.

"Selling newspapers, sonny?" asked an old man. He smiled at me kindly.

I wanted to tell him what I thought of his stupid question, but I just muttered, "Yes, sir." My pale breath puffed from my raw lips.

"Let me have one. Here's a dime." He had flowing white mustaches; he reminded me of General Bullmoose from "Li'l Abner."

I gave the old man the driest paper in the pile. His gnarled fingers clutched the little silver coin the way a mama vulture might hold a still-squirming mouse she had captured for her hungry brood. The ancient gentleman shared a secret smile with his chauffeur. I reached forward for the dime, and the old man dropped it into my numb hand. I couldn't hold onto it, and the dime fell into the slush. I knelt quickly to retrieve it, and just then the black car sped off around the corner, spraying me from head to toe with the filthiest, coldest, wettest gunk in the world. Melting Ohio slush has properties liquid helium can only *dream* about. I was miserable. I never saw that car again; I never found that damn dime in the puddle of slush, either. Yet that chance encounter on a freezing day in Cleveland was to change my life. That old gentleman had been Jules Verne.

I've never told this story before, but it's the primary reason that I write science fiction. I've always felt that the genre promised me something on that fateful afternoon, and I'm going to keep at it until I get that blessed dime back. I learned then, at an age when other boys are spinning tops and rolling hoops, that the life of a writer is fraught both with blessings and curses, and that very often they come mixed inextricably. I think the reason some people collaborate on fiction (or get married) is to shuck the curses off on someone else and keep the blessings. I can't swear for certain; but at one time or another I've done both things, and my experience has led me with the force of inescapable logic to a maxim, or great truth: You can't beat the house. I will hastily admit that this thought is not original with me; nevertheless, I think I've made a hard-won discovery or two that I might pass along, to indicate where the unwary science-fiction writer might hedge his bets. It is not always clear in this rigged flat store of a world who the house is, or even what the stakes are.

The foregoing will suggest to the reader that the honest writer must defend himself, that the creative process is in some sense an adversary situation. I insist that this is true, although for each individual writer the source and the amount of adversity differ. Adversity is a natural part of artistic creation of any sort, because there is an essential tension built in, the conflict that comes from the constant need to make choices. Should the writer, or painter, or composer leave the work as it is, or add another touch, or take something away? This internal struggle is a great source of adversity in many forms, but for now it will be simpler to mention a more readily identifiable form: other people involved in the publishing industry, whose interests are similar to the writer's but not identical.

I can recall remarkably well the day my first novel was accepted. The letter from the publisher takes up the first page in my rather thin scrapbook. I was filled with all the wild and uproarious emotion you might expect, at least for several hours. Later, however, I began to look over the contract I had been offered. At this stage of my career, without an agent, I had no idea of the contest of wills that printed form represented. I lived not far from New York City at this period, and so I called the publisher, Cipher Books (not their real name) and made a lunch date with my editor, X (not his or her real name). You must remember that I had as yet no idea of the subtle interplay that develops between author and editor, or the ways that a writer may learn just where he stands in relation to his adversary.

135

And never doubt that this *is* an adversary situation. One of my favorite people, an editor at a later version of Cipher Books, warned me once that however close a writer and an editor might become personally, the editor is always the company's man. When it's fourth and inches near the goal line, the editor is not going to let you sneak across just because you've been great pals in the past. That is a hard lesson to learn, and I doubt if it's possible to become truly successful in science fiction—or any other genre—unless it is learned.

Well, that first lunch was very enlightening. Very enlightening, indeed. I wish some of the *How to Get Your Junk Published* books that crowd the shelves in bookstores would give some hints about managing such things as standing up for your own rights when you don't have the faintest idea what they may be. I met X promptly at noon. That is, I encountered a secretary stationed in a plush foyer; she sat there like one of the Eumenides with a part-time job. She really didn't like the way I looked at all. Thirteen years ago I tended toward boots and jeans and turtleneck sweaters—hell, I dress exactly the same way today—and when I said I was there to see X, the secretary gave me just the coolest hint of a smile.

She picked up her phone. "X?" she said. "There's some delivery boy here for you, but he isn't carrying anything. Was I supposed to give him something? There's nothing on my desk."

"Excuse me," I tried to explain. I was waved to silence.

X apparently told the secretary that no delivery boy was expected, and the secretary hung up the phone. Her glance turned colder; I had better have some good explanation for wasting their time. I was disturbing the sacred halls where many people were employed in turning literature into mere books.

"I have a lunch appointment," I said. I think I was pretty meek by this time. That was how that secretary was supposed to make me feel.

Her eyes grew wider; suddenly, like a rosebud opening in time-lapse photography, comprehension grew upon her. "Oh," she said, "you're an author." She spoke that last word the way some other person might have said "weevil." "Your name?" I told her; she dialed X again and relayed the information. "X will be right out," she said. Then she looked away, at nothing in particular; I was no longer even so interesting as a delivery boy.

X came out, hearty and smiling and hiding with expert skill the immediate impression he must had of me. "Let's go," said X, "I know a great place not far from here."

My excitement returned in full force, now that I was known for who I was—not a delivery boy at all, but a genuine science-fiction writer. I was all set for some literary high-life. I didn't expect the round table at the Algonquin, of course, but at that point I was tingling just to be riding up and down in the same elevators that had carried some of the most famous writers in the world. My imagination buoyed me along until we got to the Bun 'n' Burger and I realized that, no, I was not going to be entertained in the same style as, say, Fred Mustard Stewart. I took my stool at the counter, and said very little during the brief lunch.

Afterward, back in the offices of Cipher Books, when we had wound our way around to X's own cubicle, I sat uneasily beside the editor's very cluttered desk.

"I brought my contract," I said. "There are just a couple of things I'd like to ask about it."

"Of course," said X, settling his spectacles on the end of his nose and gazing at me with a kind of fond, paternal interest.

"Well," I began nervously, "it's mostly about the advance." I had checked the current volume of *Writer's Market*, and it said very explicitly there that Cipher Books's minimum advance was Y dollars. The advance my contract called for was Y minus five hundred dollars. "Well, I'd like a little more, sir." I got this horrible feeling that I had suddenly become Oliver Twist, and that I was going to be thrashed and tossed into a cold cell to spend the night.

I was wrong. X's expression never changed. It remained calm and pleasant. "No," he said simply.

"But *Writer's Market—*"

"Y minus five hundred dollars is our customary advance for a first novel. Now, were there any other problems?"

I did have a few. Never having looked at a contract before, I didn't know exactly what I was getting into, of course; but even I could tell when I was getting shafted. I decided to go along with most of it and not make trouble because, after all, I was thrilled to death that they were going to publish my book. But I pointed out three or four places where I felt they had overstepped the bounds of civility by making their thievery just a little too blatant.

"Fine," said X, "we'll just strike this clause here. But I'll have to add this, and this, too. It's all standard, don't worry. This is our standard way of handling this."

And you know, he was telling the truth, too. The contract was like the Hydra; every unfavorable phrase I eliminated was replaced by two more, each more abstrusely worded than the last. I finally gave up and just signed the son of a bitch, which was Cipher's strategy all along.

Please allow me to make it clear that this kind of difficulty is about the simplest and least hazardous adversity a science-fiction writer must face. Overcoming it is what agents are for.

Yet we all know that once a contract is signed, relations with the editor have not ended. Not by a long sight. Several years later, after I had established myself as someone who finished the novels he contracted for in a generally publishable fashion, I sold a mainstream novel to a third incarnation of Cipher Books. The editor there, another X, happened to be the father of a well-known television personality, and spent the whole time I was in his company regaling me with show-biz gossip and clever stuff he had said to Gerald Ford and his recollections of Ernest Hemingway. I was made to understand that this was a Big Time Editor. That might well have been Maxwell Perkins's own pencil sharpener mounted on that desk.

Anyway, this X liked me even less than the previous X had. I was made to sit down quietly while X took his position in a comfortable reclining chair. His desk was not cluttered; this editor had underlings to take care of trivial matters like correspondence, contracts, and manuscripts. The most visible objects in the office were the squash racquets leaning against a bookcase. I immediately understood something: this man was something of an elitist. A typical New York businessman who went out for some exercise on his lunch hour or after work might have had racquetball equipment or tennis stuff. The squash racquets loudly signaled Ivy League, and they were intentionally conspicuous. On X's desk was a ceramic mug with his school's crest on it and X's year of graduation.

All of this stuff was getting me riled because, as it happened, I went to the same university, and I was always pretty good at whopping squash balls around, myself. I just react badly to this business of being categorized on sight by editors and agents and publishers and salesmen; it galls me even worse when the same thing is done to my fiction. So I kind of slipped it into the conversation that I had gone to X's alma mater;

once he understood this, his attitude toward me changed. He realized instantly that I must have been one of those wretched scholarship cases. X leaned toward me in a conspiratorial manner and gave me a single piece of advice.

"George," he said, very seriously, "remember, this isn't *science fiction* you're writing now. You're just going to have to do the best job you can, and then I'll fix it up."

That steamed me but good. I felt obliged to make a few pertinent points about the literary excellence of science fiction on our best days, something he evidently knew nothing about, but he didn't give me the chance. I got about three words out of my mouth when he interrupted me, blithely shooing me out of the office and telling me to run along. So I went home and wrote the goddamn book.

The next time I saw X was after I delivered the novel and he had read it. Once more he welcomed me into his tidy domain, which was still free of the litter and dross of the book-churning business. He sat behind his desk and looked at me with evident satisfaction.

"Well," he said, "I read it, and to tell the truth, I liked it."

I was startled, but happy. "Great," I said.

"Yes, I really liked it."

"Wow," I said.

"Except for one thing."

"Uh, oh," I said.

X nodded his head sagely. This is a trick they learn only through experience; I've had sage editors and unsage editors. "You have just one little problem," he advised me with all the sageness at his command. "You haven't killed off enough people."

That took me by surprise. The book was kind of a disaster novel, and I'd worked out appropriate fates for each of the major and minor characters. X was making it sound as if I had a quota of bodies to meet. My confusion must have been evident.

X smiled. "It's a tiny matter, we can fix it up this afternoon. Just pick any other character, anybody at all, and kill him some way."

I felt myself getting testy. "Look," I said, "the people who live through the book all learn something, or their lives are changed in some meaningful way, and if I killed one of them now it would spoil the whole—"

"I want one of them *muerto* in the next thirty minutes," said X sternly. "You can use the typewriter in the next office."

I picked up my manuscript and went into the other room. I sat and stared at the typewriter for a few minutes. No editor in my whole career had ever had the temerity to mess with the internal structure of one of my books like this. If I hadn't been so intimidated by the fact that I was working outside our comfortable science-fiction neighborhood, I might have rebelled more strongly. But this was my first dip in the mainstream, and some part of my mind argued that X knew better than I about mainstream standards.

All right, I told myself, I'll do it; but I'll kill the poor bastard in the dumbest, most ridiculous way I can think of. The book was about a hurricane, so I had one of the lesser characters go outside and get bonked in the head by a loose-flying plastic lawn flamingo. I came back into X's office with the two pages of typescript; he glanced at them briefly. "Terrific," he said, and inserted them into the novel.

Because of that experience, my friends have been giving me flamingo figurines and flamingo stationery and flamingo ashtrays and other flamingo stuff until my living room looks like a bird sanctuary. I'm kind of glad I put that scene in there, because now I think it's funny as hell; but I'll be doggoned if I understand why it makes the novel better.

I will repeat that this may sound like aggravation, rather than real adversity. On the face of it, that's true. It becomes adversity after years of tedious repetition, when every book represents a battle-to-come over some unpredictable snag. In those contests, the editor always has the home-field advantage and always wins the toss of the coin. Why do editors always feel they have to demonstrate how vigilant and meticulous they are? Do they think we won't respect them unless they pretend to do a little editing? There's an old proverb that sums it up neatly if crudely: the head cook won't okay the soup unless he can pee in the pot himself. I'd like to know where the proverb comes from—Estonia or Bhutan or someplace like that—so that I'll stay out of their restaurants.

Before I leave the discussion of editors, I'd like to make a couple of remarks. The first is that the editor of this volume, Sharon Jarvis, was my editor at two different publishing houses, and under no circumstances would I want anyone to suspect that she might be one of the Editor Xs I've described. Sharon is a pussycat, a perceptive but not intrusive editor, and pretty darn sage in her own right.

The second thing is that I made a little outline to myself when I began this essay. I divided the sources of adversity into three types. My list looked like this:

1. Other people: editors
   agents
   other writers
   readers
   family and friends
2. Outside influences
3. The writer himself

My plan was to divide the requested fifteen or twenty manuscript pages into three equal parts. However, I see that it is already page 12 and all I've managed to do is the first 20 per cent of the opening third. So I will simply consign agents, other writers, readers, and family and friends to hell and move on. I had no idea that the subject of editors would make me so vehement. I should have begun with someone else, and given a broader overview of anguish. Yet I suppose the reader gets the general idea.

I just know the same thing is going to happen again here in *Part Two: Outside Influences*. My list contains six of them, from rent to particular vices. None of them, however, threatens so much adversity as the single representative I choose to examine now.

The IRS. Let me tell you about the time I was snared.

Now, if you're a science-fiction writer full time, without any other source of income, the world goes out of its way to make things tough for you. You learn early on in the game that standardized forms aren't equipped to handle the kinds of answers you give. Low-level office workers are perplexed about how to deal with you; that's the dangerous part. *Never* get a low-level office worker perplexed; you can end up in the most god-awful places.

I remember once when I was taken to the emergency room of a hospital that treats a large number of low-income people for free. Before I could be attended to, a clerical worker had to decide if I was there as a paying customer or otherwise.

"How much money do you earn a week?" she asked me.

I really wasn't feeling up to going through this, because I had an inkling of what was coming. "I don't earn by the week," I said, groaning. "I write for a living."

"Oh," she said brightly, "then how much do you make a month? I'll just divide by four."

"Won't work, either. I get a big chunk of money when I sell a book idea to a publisher, and another big chunk when I deliver it. Nothing in between." I knew better than to mention the little dribs and drabs of cash that are the unexpected dividends of a writer's life, plus the money I make irregularly when I turn out a short story or two. The lady was having enough trouble with the main factors.

Finally she went over to her supervisor. The two of them came back to me and looked me over as if I was running some kind of short con game.

"What does he do?" asked the supervisor.

"He says he writes," said the clerk.

"Just put down 'unemployed,'" said the supervisor disgustedly.

She went away, and the clerk was pleased to have the matter resolved for her. The best part of it was that I was treated for free. Sing ho! for the life of a scribbler.

It doesn't always work out that way, however. When the IRS called me in, I was naturally very nervous. I wondered what kind of mistake I had made, and I pictured all sorts of doom hanging over me, everything up to and including Leavenworth. I showed up on the appointed morning, waited until my name was called, and followed the tax representative to her cubicle (it seems to me that I spend a lot of my life following people into cubicles. It makes you wonder if, just to even things up once in a while, you ought to get your own cubicle, and then they would have to come looking for you). (Well, in the case of the IRS, they *would* come looking, and they'd find you pretty fast, too.)

My auditor's name was Miss X. She was polite and pleasant and not at all the way I imagined a tax inquisitioner to be. She allayed my doubts and fears at once. "Oh, there's probably nothing terribly wrong with your form," she said. "Your name just came up in our random audit."

Swell, I thought, because *I* am ready for *you*. A science-fiction writer gets a lot of breaks, taxwise, because so many things can be legally deducted. All the books I use for research, for instance, and that portion of my rent that represents my office space. Not to mention all the gin and tonics consumed in the company of anybody even tangentially connected with publishing. This makes a writer's tax form more complicated to fill out; you have to itemize, you have to include extra things like the Self-Employment Tax, and you have to show a little imagination sometimes in labeling your deductions. If one of those hard-nosed auditors ever went to a science-fiction convention and saw what goes on there, he'd probably be less inclined to have the federal government pay for my participation: travel, meals, and good old *Misc.*

I keep a day-by-day ledger of all my expenses, income, and deductions. I keep all my receipts for the year in separate envelopes according to category, and come income tax time I total them all up and fill in the blanks. It took me a couple of years to learn to ask for all those receipts everywhere I went; but sitting at the auditor's desk, I was glad I was fully armed with them. I could account for every penny on that return.

"So you're a writer?" said X.

"Yes."

"Ever had anything published?" (My God, do I *hate* that question. Why do so many people ask me that when I tell them what I do? I know; it's because I look like a delivery boy.)

"Yes," I said.

She glanced through the forms, checked the stacks of receipts and canceled checks, and was just about to dismiss me back into the free world when she noticed something. "This isn't actually a W-2 form you have here," she said.

I forget what the actual designation is; it's a form I get yearly from my agent, with basically all the same information that a regular W-2 form has.

"No," I said, "I guess not." I couldn't see what the trouble was.

She pointed it out. "It's headed 'Rents and Royalties.' "

"Uh, huh," I said. "I'm paid on a royalty basis. A percentage of the cover price of each book sold."

She understood that easily enough; she was a bright lass. "Then you have to fill out form so-and-so," she said.

I have never heard of form so-and-so, and I told her. She was nice enough to get one for me. She began to explain it, and very quickly I realized that she had made an error. This form did not relate to my situation at all. The IRS defines "royalty" in two ways, and she was using the wrong way: royalties are also what a corporation, say, Exxon, might pay for leasing oil land.

I tried to make her understand the confusion. "That doesn't apply to me," I said. "It wouldn't be fair, in the first place. It's making me pay tax on the same money I paid the Self-Employment Tax on. I pay that *instead* of form so-and-so."

X sighed; her job must be a constant, daily, hourly hassle with people over just this sort of thing. Still, I found that I had little sympathy. She turned to a shelf behind her, which held a long row of thick books. The Tax Laws. She pulled down a volume and paged through it, finally finding a section she liked. She began to read aloud. The words made no sense.

"I don't understand any of that," I said.

She read it a second time, but it didn't help. It occurred to me that the Tax Laws are like the *I Ching*, the Chinese Book of Changes. The message encoded in the esoteric language reveals more about the soul of he who looks into the book, than of the book itself or those who composed it. It was like appearing before the Oracle of Apollo at Delphi: you took your life in your own hands just to ask a question.

We realized after about thirty minutes that we'd reached an impasse. X did the appropriate thing; she made all the necessary notations on my file and told me that it would be sent up a level to her supervisor. I'd be notified of The Decision. I left feeling a little weak and shaky, because this matter might well cost me a lot of money.

So I waited. And waited. Many weeks later, I received a notice from the IRS saying that because I hadn't appeared for my audit, they were fining me a whole pile of money and demanded my appearance once again, "Oh, boy," I muttered, "here comes the computer foul-up."

And that's just what it was, too. There was no record that I'd ever come in to talk to X. I killed another afternoon going through the whole business all over again with Miss Y—the IRS has a policy of rotating their employees to prevent job burnout; it means that the rep you talked to the first time won't be there the second time. Y was easily persuaded that I had, in fact, made my first appearance, because I had documentary evidence in my possession from X. Y apologized for the trouble and told me not to worry, and to ignore the fine. It would be taken off my record.

If I had only grown up to work in a Dairy Queen, all of this would have been simpler. I won't have to tell the astute reader that this thing just got worse. My first file, the lost one, was found and I had to go through an appeal process, meanwhile accruing interest on the disputed tax from form so-and-so plus the fine (which hadn't been removed) plus late penalties and another fine. Then the second file, from Y, turned up and wanted to know why, if I was being fined for not filing form so-and-so, there was no such form in my file? The answer seemed obvious to me, but then I make my living dealing with the fantastic.

This went on for two years. I could not make the IRS realize that they had two active files covering the same situation with different information and opposing interpretations. One or the other kept surfacing; I made visit after visit to the federal building, meeting many varied and interesting people on those occasions, never the same one twice. I had to start over again, from the top, at each appointment. Some of the auditors had a tough time understanding what it was all about; a few of them couldn't get past the paradox that although I owned no real estate, I was apparently leasing valuable mineral rights or something to some undisclosed second party.

At last I was informed that I lost my appeal (I don't remember ever taking part in it). I was presented with a bill for a figure six times what the original form so-and-so levy had been. And the IRS wanted their money *fast*. Their next option was seizure of property. I laughed at that; my most valuable possession is the typewriter I'm using now, and it's ten years old. I don't have a car or a stereo. I scoffed at their threat. Then they made it clear to me that they had plenty of other options, and now Leavenworth was no longer so far-fetched a destination.

All because Miss X, who had disappeared as completely as the night-before-last, had chosen her own special reading of the word "royalty," and because Miss Y had begun a file that flickered in and out of existence like some new, theoretical sub-atomic particle. All because I write science fiction to earn my keep, and my life can't be squeezed into the little spaces they have on their forms.

There is adversity that strengthens one to oppose, that builds character and will. The IRS is another matter, however, and struggling against it leads only to frustration and, eventually, madness. I wish I could end this section with a tidy, clever anecdote, but the business is still unsettled; I'm still being called down to the IRS office. They may become a lifetime hobby. I would have been smarter just to tell them that the hospital staff said I was unemployed, then let the two sets of clerks battle it out. . . .

And that's all that I want to say about the second source of adversity, those forces entirely beyond the writer's control that just want to screw around with him on general principles. The bad news is that in the long run, of course, adversity (I mean Adversity) cannot be overcome. The best you can hope for is a little more time, a standing eight-count before someone throws in the towel and you're TKO'ed right into the Long Goodbye. The good news is that this is precisely the Human Condition, and that is the very thing that writers are in existence to document. Without it, we'd have to apprentice ourselves out as millers and wheelwrights and ship chandlers. It is good, however, that the writer is not constantly faced with this sort of adversity, the Life and Death stuff. If that were true, what fool would waste his time in a burning building typing up lyrical lines describing the flaming pages of his own manuscript?

I see, at this late point, that I must abandon somewhat an initial resolve. That is, I was determined to finish this essay without going into any particular detail about just why I was chosen, of all my colleagues, to wrestle with this subject. I suppose I must sketch in the situation just a little, so that the reader may appreciate just how fortunate I've been. I wanted to keep things light and jolly, mocking a few of my own foibles; but I can't do that and still attempt the very serious point I wish to make. So please bear with me while I fill in some recent history.

In January of 1975, with my writing career about four years old and rolling right along, I developed a serious abdominal condition which required surgery to remove several large growths. Nothing terribly unprecedented about the situation; it happens to lots of people. I had no hospitalization, however, and when I got out of the hospital I forked over a few thousand dollars in cash. I would have preferred going to Europe that spring, but what the hell; instead I stayed home and played some basketball, stretching and strengthening myself. The tumorous condition recurred in the fall; once more I spent several weeks in the hospital, losing work time, missing deadlines, getting perilously thin, and learning to appreciate Demerol. When I was discharged this time, though, I didn't have the four grand to give the hospital, so I signed my first promissory note.

The medical condition, as tedious as it is uncomfortable, has recurred several more times. By now, I've spent so long in the hospital for surgery, procedures, treatments, therapies, tests, and false alarms that it seems that most of my life is wasted in the repair shop, with my warranty expired. Meanwhile, like a snowstorm off Lake Erie, the bills have been drifting deeper and deeper.

Now, if I had been a bookstore clerk—as I was in my youth—I could not have kept my job. What kind of position *could* I have had? How could I have supported myself? Even now, between operations, I have intermittent episodes every few weeks that confine me to bed for several days at a stretch. As a writer I don't have to worry about calling in sick all the time; I can work during those blessed weeks when I'm free of pain. Then I turn out as much as I can get done, and love every second of it.

When I'm ill, I read and plan and make outlines of stories I can't wait to write.

That's only part of my point: a writer has freedom, a certain flexibility to work when it is most convenient for him. Without this liberty, the last several years would have been much more frightening. But I intend to go further: as a *science fiction* writer, as a member of a genre, I have been given even more help in keeping the various wolves at bay. Please realize that those earlier tales of woe I related, and all the ones I skipped, were happening concurrently, while I was often too ill to give them my full attention. Time after time, science fiction—our ghetto, I've heard it called; but it seems more like a neighborhood to me, in all the special senses of the word—provided a support I found completely missing in the broader and colder precincts of the literary world. I don't claim that I was given undue consideration, or that editors ever compromised their integrity to help me out. My bad stories are routinely returned, with regrets. (I will acknowledge that certain editors have done me the favor of speeding up their usual reply time, knowing that my creditors have long since lost patience.) I can think of nowhere else, possibly in no other genre, where I could have kept myself afloat as well. I don't have to starve in a garret until I complete a literary novel that might not even be accepted. The commercial mechanism of science fiction is more responsive than that.

Science fiction has always been willing to welcome the new writer, the unknown name, the first novelist. I write an odd kind of science fiction, and I've developed a moderate audience; I wouldn't say that I'm one of the most popular or best-selling authors in the science-fiction world. Nevertheless, there is room for me to try out my particular point-of-view, alongside all the other varied and mixed-together sorts of fantasy and science fiction available today. I suspect that in the mainstream, without a sizable commercial success, my writing career might have been over a few books ago. The knowledge that I have been allowed to carve a little niche for myself in the science-fiction environment has helped greatly to bear me up through the frustrating and despairing moments.

And I haven't said a word yet about the emotional support I've received from my friends in the science-fiction world. The hardest thing about serious adversity, I think, is the sense of isolation that develops. Sometimes this loneliness is exaggerated in your mind, but that doesn't make it any the less potent. Our genre had been unfailingly generous in spirit, patient and understanding with me when I have been ill and incommunicative. I have nothing but gratitude for all those people, science-fiction pros and fans alike, who have offered me encouragement and help.

Recently I have read some interviews in the *Writers at Work* series published by Penguin Books. A question was asked of several of the great expatriate writers who lived in Paris in the 1920s: did they, at that time, have a feeling of being an American community of writers? The frequent answer was no; they saw each other now and then, gossiped, talked about their work, but they never really felt like a *community*.

Well, at the risk of sounding too sentimental, I wouldn't trade my crazy memories of science-fiction convention weekends—with *our* community—for a month of Sundays with the Lost Generation.

Unless they maybe threw in a couple of Folies girls and a case of Veuve Clicquot, too. And then only maybe.